LINCOLN CHRISTIAN

W9-CBW-468

"Can Mormons and Calvinist evangelicals talk to each other without compromising their beliefs or minimizing their differences? Richard Mouw knows the pitfalls but shows it can be done. The engaging story of his decade-long conversation with Mormons is a model for interfaith dialogue in the twenty-first century and an exemplification of Christian love, intelligence, and good humor."

— RICHARD BUSHMAN
Columbia University

"I have had the privilege of partnering with Rich Mouw in the Evangelical-Mormon dialogues he describes in this little book. It always amazes me how some who have not been a part of these conversations can confidently pronounce on what really happened at them and even on the motives of the participants. Rich sets the story straight here.... A must-read for anyone interested in Latter-day Saints!"

— CRAIG L. BLOMBERG
Denver Seminary

Talking with Mormons

An Invitation to Evangelicals

Richard J. Mouw

WILLIAM B. EERDMANS PUBLISHING COMPANY

GRAND RAPIDS, MICHIGAN / CAMBRIDGE, U.K.

© 2012 Richard J. Mouw
All rights reserved

Published 2012 by
Wm. B. Eerdmans Publishing Co.
2140 Oak Industrial Drive N.E., Grand Rapids, Michigan 49505 /
P.O. Box 163, Cambridge CB3 9PU U.K.

Printed in the United States of America

17 16 15 14 13 12   7 6 5 4 3 2 1

Library of Congress Cataloging-in-Publication Data

Mouw, Richard J.
Talking with Mormons: an invitation to Evangelicals / Richard J. Mouw.
       p.   cm.
ISBN 978-0-8028-6858-9 (pbk.: alk. paper)
1. Evangelicalism — Relations — Church of Jesus Christ of Latter-day Saints.
2. Evangelicalism — Relations — Mormon Church. 3. Church of Jesus Christ
of Latter-day Saints — Relations — Evangelicalism. 4. Mormon Church —
Relations — Evangelicalism. 5. Evangelicalism. 6. Church of Jesus Christ
of Latter-day Saints — Doctrines. 7. Mormon Church — Doctrines.   I. Title.

BR1641.M67M68   2012
289.3   dc23

2012009876

www.eerdmans.com

Contents

—◦◦◦◦—

126735

Acknowledgments

———◦◦◦———

Authors frequently name, at the beginning of the book, the people whose support and input have made their projects possible. But the writers then typically add something like this: "In the final analysis, though, I alone am to be held responsible for the views set forth here."

I also owe much to many people. But given the somewhat controversial character of the subject matter of this book, I don't want to implicate friends who might suffer from guilt by association. It must suffice, then, simply to express gratitude for dialogue partners who have taught me much during the journey that brought me to the point of writing this book. In the final analysis, though, I do take full personal responsibility for what gets said in these pages.

One acknowledgment, however, is necessary. For over a decade now the Stewardship Foundation in Tacoma, Washington, has provided generous support for Fuller's involvement in this particular dialogue, as well as in other interfaith and "civility" projects. The Stewardship Foundation was established by

Acknowledgments

C. Davis Weyerhaeuser for the purpose of supporting "Christ-centered organizations that share their faith in Jesus in word and deed with others throughout the world." Dave Weyerhaeuser was a gifted and creative evangelical leader, and I am deeply grateful that the Foundation that continues to carry out his vision sees this kind of "dialogic evangelicalism" as a way of serving that overall goal.

Explaining the Sound Bites

———❧———

After giving out dozens of sound bites about Mormonism during the buildup to the 2012 presidential election, I decided it was time to write a book on the subject. Mitt Romney has been much in the news, and journalists have been eager to find someone who was willing to offer some thoughts about how evangelicals might end up voting if their only choice was between President Obama and a Mormon.

At least one prominent fundamentalist preacher had announced during the primary season that because Mormonism is a cult, no Mormon should ever be allowed to occupy the Oval Office. In my interviews with journalists, I offered an alternative evangelical perspective. A dozen years of sustained dialogues with Mormon scholars and church leaders have convinced me that the "cult" label does not apply accurately to the Church of Jesus Christ of Latter-day Saints. Not that I'm ready to give them a free pass as simply another Christian denomination. I have too many serious theological disagreements with Mormonism to offer that verdict. But Mormons don't deserve to be dismissed by Christians as a cult. Scientology, in my view, is a cult. The Jehovah's Witnesses belong to a cult. Hare Krishna is a cult. But present-day Mormonism should not be lumped together with those groups.

My Mormon friends admire Billy Graham. They read C. S. Lewis for spiritual inspiration. They write insightful commentaries on the Epistle to the Romans. Of course, all of that is mixed in with many things that I find worrisome. But we have been able to talk about the worrisome things. And I thank God for that.

But back to the sound bites. Anyone who has been interviewed frequently by journalists can testify to the fact that after an hour of detailed conversation the only thing that actually shows up in the published article from all that you said is — at best — a few sentences. Not that I resent that. I find the journalists whose primary assignment is religious topics to be highly informed and intelligent people. They regularly express their disappointment that the word limits they must honor keep them from covering their subject matter in the way they would like. When I see what they've done with the opinions I've offered at some length, I seldom feel that I've been misrepresented.

But I do often worry about having my thoughts being *under*-represented. And that has certainly been the case with regard to my sound bites about Mormonism.

I'm not conscious of having approached the writing of this short book in a defensive mood. It's simply that as a teacher I haven't felt that I've been given the opportunity to engage in adequate teaching on the subject. So this book is my effort to take a little more space than I've been given elsewhere, to elaborate on a few sentences here and there that have been given public exposure.

On the other hand, I've already noted that this is a short book. I do think that some longer books are necessary on the subject from an evangelical perspective. I don't know whether I'll ever write one of those longer books. If I were to do it, though, I would want to dig more deeply into Mormon theology than I do in these pages. And I would want also to dig more deeply into my own theology as a part of that longer discussion. In doing so, I would give more detailed evidence to what I can only testify to briefly here, namely that I approach my engagement with Mormonism as a Calvinist. I believe in a sovereign God. I am convinced of the utter depravity of our fallen condition. I look to Jesus Christ alone for my salvation — because he did for sinners like me what we could never do for ourselves, paying the debt for our guilt and shame on the Cross of Calvary.

I haven't succeeded in convincing my Mormon friends that they ought wholeheartedly to embrace those Calvinist convictions. But they've been willing to hear me out. And sometimes — not always, but sometimes — they even sound as though they're moving in the direction of some of the key convictions that are for me rooted in my Calvinism. In turn, I've been willing to hear them out as they've responded to my questions and probings. Furthermore, we keep getting back together for more discussions of these matters — topics that we agree are of eternal importance. In all of that, it has never felt to me as though I was talking to members of a "cult." Which is why I sense the obligation to explain in a little detail here why I see these conversations as important ones.

Tabernacle Apology

—⚬⚬⚬—

On Sunday evening, November 14, 2004, I stood behind a podium in the center of the platform at the Mormon Tabernacle in Salt Lake City. My assignment was to welcome the standing-room-only audience of both Latter-day Saints (LDS) and Protestant evangelicals who had gathered for what had been billed as "An Evening of Friendship" between the two communities.

The idea for the event originated when my good friend, the Mormon theologian Robert Millet, called to tell me he had found out that the evangelical apologist Ravi Zacharias was going to be speaking in Utah, and Bob wanted to invite Ravi to speak at Brigham Young University as well. If Ravi agreed to the visit, Bob said, it would be good if I'd be present to introduce Ravi by way of framing the event as a next step in our ongoing Mormon-evangelical dialogue. I liked the idea a lot and promised to do what Bob was asking.

A few days later, Bob called again. He had checked the idea out with the LDS leadership and they had expressed willingness to make the Tabernacle in Salt Lake City available for Ravi to speak about "Jesus Christ: The Way, the Truth, and the Life," with both evangelicals and Mormons invited to attend. That sounded even better to me, and I was pleased when Bob soon informed me that Ravi had accepted the invitation. With the approval of the LDS leadership, he was asked simply to set forth the basic message of the Christian gospel — with the only stipulation being that he not engage in any anti-Mormon polemics in his presentation.

Ravi came through beautifully on the appointed evening, and it was a thrill for me to be able to participate in the program. My only regret was that, in the aftermath, my own introductory remarks, lasting a mere seven minutes, came to dominate the news reports, drawing some angry criticisms of the whole evening from some evangelical quarters.

Here's what stirred up the storm. I apologized to Mormons for the way we evangelicals have often treated them. Having engaged in serious dialogue about doctrinal matters with some Mormon scholars for the previous six years, I said, I continue to believe that we disagree about matters "of eternal importance." At the same time, however, I was "now convinced that we evangelicals have often seriously misrepresented the beliefs and practices of the Mormon community" — to the point, I added, of sinning against Mormonism.

I'm not going to defend that apology here. It simply stands as I stated it. But I do want to explain why I am minded to reach out to Mormons in a conciliatory way. Some of us from the evangelical community see ourselves as having reached a new stage in our relationships with Latter-day Saints. We've been involved in extensive dialogue for more than a decade now; and together, Mormons and evangelicals, we have been going out of our way genuinely to listen carefully to each other, trying to get a clearer understanding of what the real differences are between us.

And we are all agreed that there are indeed some big differences. I am not a relativist who believes anything goes in theology. I care deeply about what I take to be the basic issues of life, especially when it comes to questions like "Who is God?" and "What does it take for a person to get right with God?" And I can't get far into a discussion of those questions without talking about Jesus as the heaven-sent Savior who went to the Cross of Calvary to pay the debt for our sins and, having been raised from the dead, ascended to the heavenly throne from which he will someday return to appear on clouds of glory. I believe those things with all my heart, and I believe them because they are taught in the Bible, which is God's infallible Word to us, telling us all we need to know about God's will for our lives.

Those are the kinds of things we talk about together — Mormons and evangelicals — in our friendly exchanges. To be sure, the discussions have had their ups and downs. Sometimes we evangelicals think we and the Mormons are very far apart, and then there are other times when it appears that we're not quite as far apart as we had imagined. We want to keep pushing our Mormon friends to help us better understand their answers. This isn't just a matter of being nice to Mormons. It's really about being obedient to God. He has told us not to bear false witness against our neighbors, and it is important for our own spiritual health not to misrepresent what our Mormon neighbors believe.

I'm not going to give any kind of detailed account here of the substance of our dialogues. Several excellent books have been published in recent years that show evangelicals and Mormons actually engaged in friendly but probing exchanges.[1] This short book offers some personal reflections on what has been going on. I provide them in part to respond to some criticisms that have been aired about our endeavors. But even more, I hope what I say here can at least do a little bit to change the atmosphere in Mormon-evangelical relations. I'm under no delusions about putting all of the evangelical worries to rest. But I do sense a need to provide some explanations about why some of us see this endeavor as important to pursue.

1. Craig L. Blomberg and Stephen E. Robinson, *How Wide the Divide? A Mormon and an Evangelical in Conversation* (Downers Grove: InterVarsity Press, 1997); Robert L. Millet and Gregory C. V. Johnson, *Bridging the Divide: The Continuing Conversation between a Mormon and an Evangelical* (Rhinebeck: Monkfish Publishing, 2007); Gerald McDermott and Robert L. Millet, *Claiming Christ: A Mormon-Evangelical Debate* (Grand Rapids: Brazos Press, 2007).

Adolescent Encounters

——◦◦◦◦——

War of Words

I was just entering my teens when our family traveled by car to California from our home in a town near Albany, New York. On the way we stopped in Salt Lake City and did the standard tourist thing, visiting Temple Square. Our seventh grade class had already learned a little bit about Joseph Smith and Palmyra in our required unit on New York State history, so I found the idea of a visit to the Mormon "Zion" mildly interesting. My interest turned to fascination, however, as we left Salt Lake City and headed further west.

In the backseat of our car I sat reading "Joseph Smith Tells His Own Story," a pamphlet summarizing the official version of the Mormon founder's First Vision narrative. For me, the most intriguing part of the story was his description of his state of mind just before his account of the visitation that he claimed to have experienced. As a fourteen-year-old boy, he reported, he was so distressed by "the confusion and strife among the different denominations" that it seemed "impossible for a person young as I was, and so unacquainted with men and things, to come to any certain conclusion who was right and who was wrong." The Baptists were arguing with the Presbyterians, and each in turn had their own debates with the Methodists. Everyone was intent upon proving their own views to be the right ones and the others riddled with error.

I found especially gripping Joseph Smith's poignant expression of despair: "In the midst of this war of words and tumult of opinions, I often said to myself, what is to be done? Who of all these parties are right; or, are they all wrong together? If any one of them be right, which is it, and how shall I know it?"

In the midst of his despair, Joseph discovered the passage in the Epistle of James that says, "If any of you lack wisdom, let him ask of God, that giveth to all men liberally, and upbraideth not; and it shall be given him."

It's no exaggeration to say that I felt like I had discovered a friend. Here was someone who understood my own confusions and yearnings, feelings that I had been reluctant to express to the adults in my life — and even a bit fearful of admitting to myself.

Some family background. My father had given his life to Christ in his late teens, under the influence of a fundamentalist ministry. Meeting my mother, who was of solid Dutch Calvinist stock, exposed him to Reformed Christianity. For a while he maintained his Baptist convictions, although he gradually moved in my mother's direction theologically. Eventually he studied theology and was ordained as a minister in the Reformed Church of America. Having made that move, he was fairly zealous in his defense of infant baptism, as was evident in what seemed to me as a child to be his endless (albeit always friendly) arguments on the subject with his brother, a Baptist pastor.

My impression of those debates was not unlike the experience described by the young Joseph. My dad and my uncle were each passionately sincere in their views about baptism. And each was skilled at appealing to the Bible in support of his views. Yet they disagreed, and the disagreement seemed incapable of being resolved. This disturbed me. How could I know — *really* know — whose view was the correct one?

I had become a bit of a theological debater in my own right. I had many Catholic friends around the time of our visit to Temple Square, and I would often challenge their views about going to the priest for confession and about Mary and the pope. Some of those friends were fairly articulate. I never convinced them of anything — nor did they force me to change the views that I was defending. In my private thoughts, however, this bothered me. Who was I to say that I had the "right" theology and theirs was simply wrong?

So when Joseph Smith described a time in his life as a young teenager when he was simply bewildered by "this war of words and tumult of opinions," his story resonated with me in the deep places. His teenage questions were mine as well: "Who of all these parties are right; or, are they all wrong together? If any one of them be right, which is it, and how shall I know it?"

I was not tempted to believe Joseph Smith's account of being visited by the divine Persons and angels. But, frankly, if an angel had happened to visit me with some clear answers, I would not have refused to listen.

"You're Not Even Trying to Understand!"

Two years after our visit to Salt Lake City, I sat through a series
of Sunday night talks given by a popular speaker named Walter
Martin on the subject of "the cults." By this time our family had
moved to New Jersey, and I had a small group of Christian
friends in the large public high school I was attending. Several
of them were members of the Riverdale Bible Church, and they
were excited about the series of Sunday evening lectures Martin would be giving at their church.

Walter Martin was not as well known in those days as he
would be after 1965, when he published his influential *Kingdom of the Cults.* But he was already a dynamic speaker who
could stir up an evangelical audience with his engaging sharp-
witted critiques of Mormonism, Christian Science, Jehovah's
Witnesses, and Seventh Day Adventists. (This last group he
would later remove from his list of dangerous cults.) For his
Riverdale talks he took on a specific religious movement on
each of four successive Sunday nights: Jehovah's Witnesses,
Christian Science, Seventh Day Adventists, and Mormons. I
made a point of attending the whole series.

The sessions were widely advertised, and the small church
was packed for each of the evenings. Martin was an effective
rhetorician, and I was captivated by the way he made his case
against non-Christian groups. He had a fine one-liner, for example, about Christian Science: just as Grape Nuts are neither
grapes nor nuts, Mary Baker Eddy's system of thought is neither Christian nor science.

On the evening of his talk about Mormonism the atmosphere was electric. A dozen or so Mormons were in atten-
dance, and they sat as a group near the front of the audito-

rium. We had seen them walking in, carrying their copies of the Book of Mormon. It was clear that they had come armed for debate, and Martin was eager to mix it up with them. He was in top form for his lecture.

During the discussion period, an articulate young Mormon explained that Martin had misunderstood Mormon teachings regarding atonement and salvation. Martin was not willing to yield an inch, and what began as a reasoned exchange ended in a shouting match. The young Mormon finally blurted out with deep emotion: "You can come up with all of the clever arguments you want, Dr. Martin. But I know in the depths of my heart that Jesus is my Savior, and it is only through his blood that I can go to heaven!" Martin dismissed him with a knowing smile as he turned to his evangelical audience: "See how they love to distort the meanings of words?" I am paraphrasing the preceding from a memory reaching back over about five decades, but I can still hear in my mind what the young Mormon said next, in an anguished tone: "You're not even *trying* to understand!"

I came away from that encounter convinced that Martin's theological critique of Mormonism was correct on the basic points at issue. But I also left the church that night with a nagging sense that there was more to be said, and that the way to let it be said was captured in the young Mormon's complaint: both sides had to *try* to understand each other. I hoped the day would come when I could do something to make that possible.

I've often thought of those two teenage encounters — my reading Joseph Smith's First Vision account and witnessing the exchange between Walter Martin and the young Mormon — as what really pushed me toward the study of philosophy. For one thing, the teenage Joseph Smith's question about how we can decide who is right in "this war of words and tumult of opinions" has always been high on my own intellectual agenda. On countless occasions, when I've listened to someone appeal to an inner feeling of certainty about the truth of some Christian doctrine, I have been inclined to ask, "But suppose a Mormon said that same kind of thing about an inner 'testimony' to the truth of the Book of Mormon?"

The Mormon man's poignant complaint to Walter Martin — "You're not even *trying* to understand!" — also had a lasting influence on the way I have approached disagreements about the basic issues of life. I've tried hard to understand people with whom I disagree about important issues, listening carefully to them and not resorting to cheap rhetorical tricks. Not that I've always lived up to that commitment. But it has regularly guided me in my philosophical and theological endeavors.

Moments of Healing

There's nothing I can do about the anguish of the young Mormon who, on that Sunday evening in my teenage years, pleaded for Walter Martin at least to try to understand. But our present Mormon-evangelical dialogue does at least reduce the anguish of some present-day Mormons.

Take the young woman who emailed me to tell me how moved she was when she read about the event in the Mormon Tabernacle — so moved, she said, that she wept for several minutes. In high school, she told me, her best friends were a couple of evangelical Christians. Surrounded by much secularism, they regularly talked together about their faith in Christ, and they frequently prayed together at lunchtimes in the cafeteria. But then her friends heard a guest speaker in their evangelical church denounce Mormonism as a Satan-inspired religion. The next time they were together, her friends told her they wanted nothing more to do with her. She was devastated — the most traumatic experience in her teenage years, she reported. To read about an evangelical apologizing to Mormons for sins committed against them was for her a moment of healing.

Another case, this time a middle-aged woman. She and her husband approached me after a talk I had given on a university campus. They were Mormons, they told me, and they wanted to express appreciation for the dialogue, which they had read about. "My wife wants to tell you why this is so important to us," the husband said.

She was silent for a few moments, holding back tears. Then she began. She had seen a sign in front of an evangelical church in their neighborhood, inviting women to a weekly Bible study group. "I've always wanted to learn more about the New Testament," she said, "so I started to attend. And it was wonderful!"

After the fifth weekly session, the group arranged to have lunch together, so they could learn more about each other's lives. During that time she shared with them for the first time that she was a Latter-day Saint. Suddenly, she said, the other women were noticeably cool toward her. A few days later the leader phoned to tell her that the other members had decided to ask her not to attend any longer. "I have felt so wounded," she said to me. "All I wanted was to study the Scriptures with other women who love Jesus! It means a lot to me to know that some people are working to make it possible for us to have fellowship together."

Beyond "Countercult"

———◦◦◦———

I know the approach of the "countercult" people well. I think I've read, for example, everything Walter Martin wrote about Mormonism and other "cults." I once even shared a platform with Martin, when we both spoke at a conference in Denver on the "New Age" movement. Dave Hunt — who wrote *Unmasking Mormonism* and coauthored *The Godmakers* — also spoke at that conference. Hunt insisted that C. S. Lewis's writings were infected with "pagan" ideas — he even encouraged Christian bookstore owners to stop selling Lewis's books. That was yet another occasion that reinforced my discomfort with the ways evangelicals often deal with other religious movements.

The countercult treatment of Mormonism includes a number of different strategies for attempting to discredit Mormon teaching. It will be helpful to review several of them here.

Searching for the Smoking Gun

One prominent strategy has been the search for a historical smoking gun. Mormonism is a religion that rests on some very specific (and spectacular!) historical claims. Joseph Smith claimed to have received instructions from an angel about the location of some golden plates that were buried not far from his home in Palmyra, New York. Having retrieved the plates, he translated them, producing the Book of Mormon. He also had a group of witnesses testify to having been shown the golden plates. Furthermore, throughout his lifetime he told of visions that he received in which God provided quite specific guidance for him and his followers.

And, of course, the Book of Mormon itself is set forth as a major claim to historical fact. It tells a story of ancient Israelites living on the North American continent at the time of Jesus' earthly ministry, whom the risen Christ then visited before his ascension. This detailed narrative is subject to various sorts of study — archaeological, genetic, anthropological, and the like — that could serve either to confirm or to falsify some key historical claims made by the Latter-day Saints.

All of that is important to explore in assessing Mormonism. When people base their religious convictions on claims about what really happened in the past, others have a right to see if their claims about history hold up. My own evangelical Christian convictions are subject to careful historical scrutiny. I believe Jesus really existed, that he performed miracles, that he was crucified on Calvary, that he died and then came out of the tomb as a resurrected person on Easter Sunday morning. If somehow those historical claims could be shown to be false, my faith would have been dealt a fatal blow. I take seriously what the apostle Paul says about Christ's resurrection: "If Christ has not been raised, your faith is futile and you are still in your sins" (1 Corinthians 15:17).

Historical challenges to my Christian faith, then, are fair game. And the same holds for Mormonism. When Joseph Smith "brought forth" (to use a favorite Mormon phrase) the Book of Mormon, he was setting forth a religious perspective that rises or falls on the truth of its historical accounts.

The problem with the typical evangelical historical effort to find a smoking gun in Mormon teaching is that it hasn't been very successful. In 1998 two evangelical scholars, Carl Mosser and Paul Owen, authored a lengthy essay in a journal published by Trinity Evangelical Divinity School, entitled "Mormon Scholarship, Apologetics and Evangelical Neglect: Losing the Battle and Not Knowing It?" The title summarized their story nicely. They argued that Mormon scholars had pretty much provided adequate responses to evangelical criticisms of Mormonism's historical claims. And even where those Mormon responses haven't been compelling to those of us who continue to be critical of Mormon claims, the Mormon thinkers have at least succeeded in showing that the situation is more complex than would appear from the evangelical critiques. In short, Mosser and Owen argued, "the sophistication and erudition of LDS apologetics has risen considerably while evangelical responses have not." And to make things worse, they reported, evangelicals have continued to rehearse their standard arguments against Mormonism without even demonstrating any awareness of the relevant writings by Mormon scholars.[1]

---

1. Paul Owen and Carl Mosser, "Mormon Scholarship, Apologetics and Evangelical Neglect: Losing the Battle and Not Knowing It?" *Trinity Journal* (Fall 1998): 179-205.

Does this mean that we evangelicals should give up on the investigation of Mormon historical claims? Certainly not. Mormons themselves have not backed off from a careful examination of their own nineteenth-century past or of what the Book of Mormon says about the more distant past. Anyone who looks at the kind of work being done by scholars in the Mormon History Association, for example, will see that Mormons argue among themselves about many of the topics that have a crucial bearing on how their various historical accounts stack up. The work they do should be taken seriously. A number of non-Mormon scholars have joined those discussions, and it would be good for more to sign up.

Doctrinal Checklists

A second typical countercult strategy has been the use of doctrinal checklists. What do the different groups believe about key doctrines of historic Christianity?

Start with the Trinity. Mormons deny it; so do Jehovah's Witnesses and Christian Science. How about biblical authority? Mormons and Christian Scientists have additional "revealed" books. The Jehovah's Witnesses claim the Bible alone as their authority, but they interpret it much differently than we do on key points — especially regarding the full divinity of Jesus Christ. The virgin birth of Jesus? Jehovah's Witnesses seem OK with this. Mormons claim to believe it; but, given other things they believe, is it really the same doctrine? Christian Science rejects it without any commentary necessary.

And so on. Often all of this information is actually put together in a spreadsheet type of chart of doctrines and cults. We are given the sheet so we can be aware of key points where a group in question departs from historic Christianity.

I have nothing against lists of doctrines. I regularly recite such a list in Sunday worship; here is a part of it:

I believe in the Holy Ghost;
the holy catholic church;
the communion of saints;
the forgiveness of sins;
the resurrection of the body;
and the life everlasting.

That is, of course, the final section of the Apostles' Creed. It begins with a description of what we believe about God the Father, and then goes into some detail about the person and work of Christ. After that, though, it simply offers the list I just quoted. The Nicene Creed also offers a list of things that we orthodox Christians believe — basic teachings, mentioned one after another, without a lot of commentary.

Reciting the creeds is a good thing. The lists they contain are a reminder of the essentials of the teachings we've received from the past. And that kind of recitation provides me with a helpful checklist for Christian orthodoxy. Suppose someone tells me that they agree with "just about everything in the Apostles' Creed." I'll certainly want to know what they're keeping off their "I believe" list. And I'll want to talk about the items that trouble them. Maybe they simply misunderstand what "catholic" means in the phrase "holy catholic church." Or maybe they've been misled by connotations of the word "Ghost." Or maybe they're just plain wrong about something — they understand what the church teaches and they simply disagree with it. In that case, I'll try to convince them to repair their theology!

But I have to say this also. In encouraging them to repair their theology I'll want to make sure that I have really understood their criticisms of the doctrines that I care deeply about. I'll want to know something about the context of their rejection of beliefs that I hold precious. And this is what I've come to take seriously in my dialogues with Mormons. Typically the countercult people note the doctrines that Mormons deny and then simply warn us against Mormonism on that basis. I've decided to pursue a more probing approach: to ask Mormons to clarify what it is they're denying and what teachings they're offering as an alternative to traditional Christian doctrines. One of the main reasons I've written this book is to explain why I think this is an important thing to do. More to come about this.

Demonizing

But often the countercultists take the warnings against Mormonism to even another level. They demonize Mormonism, portraying the beliefs and practices of the Latter-day Saints as "of the Devil."

I believe in the Devil and don't want in any way to underestimate his power and influence in the world. Indeed, the way I experience that power and influence most is in my own life. Satan regularly tempts me (often successfully!), luring me into bad patterns of thinking and behaving. So I take it seriously when anyone warns me against getting taken in by the Devil's wiles.

This is precisely why I want to be cautious about accusing

others of being tools of Satan. One way in which Satan tries to get at us, I'm convinced, is by getting us to go all out in attacking others. G. K. Chesterton offered wise counsel when he wrote, "Idolatry is committed, not merely by setting up false gods, but also by setting up false devils."[2] Wrongly to demonize a person who is not a demon is itself a terrible thing, and evangelicals have to be careful not to sin against Joseph Smith and his followers by setting up false devils.

I get a lot of help on this from the great Reformation theologian John Calvin. At one point in his *Institutes of the Christian Religion,* Calvin talks about what a political leader — he used the term "civil magistrate" — should be careful of when thinking about going to war against an enemy. Calvin was no pacifist. He believed that leaders, including Christian leaders, sometimes had to resort to warfare in dealing with an obvious evil. But he also knew that this is a very dangerous area spiritually. So he said that when leaders are considering initiating a military attack, they ought first of all to engage in some serious reflection. One thing leaders should do is to check out their own motives: "let them not be carried away with headlong anger, or be seized with hatred, or burn with implacable severity." And then, Calvin added, they must try as much as possible to "have pity on the common nature in the one whose special fault they are punishing."[3]

Here's what Calvin was getting at. He was aware of a sinful pattern that keeps getting stirred up in our hearts and that we

2. G. K. Chesterton, *Illustrated London News,* September 11, 1909; http://www.chesterton.org/discover/quotations.html.

3. John Calvin, *Institutes of the Christian Religion,* IV.xx.12, trans. Ford Lewis Battles, ed. John T. McNeill, Library of Christian Classics, vols. 20-21 (Philadelphia: Westminster Press, 1960).

have to be constantly on guard against: the tendency to put the best possible interpretation on our own motives and the worst possible interpretation on the motives of the people we want to attack. Recognizing the tendency, Calvin is saying that as an important spiritual exercise we should be sure to be very honest about what is going on in our own hearts, and we should be sure we're not missing something good — or at least not as bad as we're inclined to think — in the lives of the people we want to attack.

I met a pastor a while back who told me that he had used my "Whoops!" interpretation of Psalm 139 when he preached on that biblical passage the previous Sunday. I had to ask him what he meant, because I wasn't aware of having set forth a "Whoops!" interpretation. He reminded me that in one of my books I said that in Psalm 139 there is a noticeable shift of mood between what the psalmist says in verses 21-22 and what he goes on to say in verses 23-24. In those first two verses, the psalmist seems to be proclaiming boldly that he and God are on the same wavelength, working as allies in a battle against the same foes. "Do I not hate those who hate you, O Lord?" he asks. "And do I not loathe those who rise up against you? I hate them with perfect hatred. I count them my enemies."

But then, I argued in my book, his tone seems to change drastically. "This is where I talked about a 'Whoops!' moment in the psalm," the pastor said. Suddenly the psalmist seems to realize that he has slipped into an arrogant spiritual state, realizes that he has to turn inward. And that's when he pleads with the Lord to deal with the sin he finds in his own soul: "Search *me*, O God," he prays, "and know my heart; test me and know my thoughts. See if there is any wicked way in me, and lead me in the way everlasting."

I like that "Whoops!" idea. It is also what John Calvin is getting at in his discussion of going to war. We might be certain that someone is a horrible enemy who deserves all that we can use to attack him. But then there has to be that spiritual "Whoops!" moment, when we stop and reflect a bit. Am I sure I'm not getting carried away here? Have I been careful to check out everything I need to know about the person I'm planning to attack?

False Teachings, Not False Teachers

And I have to add this, too. There is a danger that when we demonize someone we feel justified in using any method we can latch onto in order to destroy the enemy. This is true in spiritual and theological struggles as well.

I once heard an evangelical leader speak out against a certain group with whom we evangelicals have significant disagreements. I happened to have studied this group's teachings in considerable detail, so I listened very carefully to how he made his case against them. Much of what he said was on target, but at one point he seriously misrepresented what the group believed.

Later I approached him privately. I told him that I admired his effort to warn his fellow Christians against the group's false teachings. But on one key point he was attributing to them something they had explicitly denied teaching. There's enough bad stuff to criticize in what the group believed, I said, without accusing them of something that's not really a part of their system.

The leader responded angrily: "You intellectuals have the

luxury of making all of these nice distinctions! But I don't have time for all your polite stuff! My job is to warn God's people against false teachers. These folks are false teachers and they don't deserve to be treated fairly!" He had a sneer on his face when he said that last word, "fairly."

This leader had adopted an anything-goes strategy in opposing a group he disagrees with. When you think about it, though, there's something very strange about that approach. We want to oppose false teachers because they teach things that aren't true. But if in our attempts to defeat them we play fast and loose with the truth, by attributing to them things that they don't in fact teach, and if we don't really care whether we have it exactly right or not, then *we* have become false teachers: teachers of untruths!

I suggest this as a rule of thumb: focus on false teachings rather than on false teachers. When we concentrate on opposing false *teachers* we tend to think about defeating *people,* which can lead to all kinds of dangers. When we concentrate on the careful examination of false *teachings* we're more aware of the need to speak truthfully.

Not that we can always separate teachings from the people who teach them. Sometimes we might misunderstand a teaching because we fail to grasp the intention of the teacher. To recognize that, though, calls for something different than a defeat-them-at-any-cost approach to real people. It requires actually making an effort to be sure we've understood the teacher and the teaching fairly.

We evangelicals make much of the importance of the Ten Commandments for public morality. I have no complaints about that. The Ten Commandments are the fundamental outline of how God wants human beings to live. To be sure, I don't know that we can enforce these Commandments in our public life today in some legal sense. Not every sin ought to be made illegal. But when we talk about what makes a society go bad we do well to focus on the Ten Commandments. Even if we can't back them up by laws, we can certainly use them in our efforts to witness to others about how the Creator wants people to behave.

Here's something to keep in mind, though. One of those Commandments tells us that God doesn't like it when we bear false witness against our neighbors. God is not honored when we're unfair to people with whom we disagree, misrepresenting what they believe. This certainly applies — I'm convinced — to our relationships with the Mormon community.

Killing a Bluebird

People who get upset with me because I don't follow the countercult line on Mormonism often tell me that I should read Walter Martin. One of them put it this way to me: "You don't need to have dialogue with Mormons to know what Mormonism is all about," he said. "All you have to do is read Walter Martin! He had those folks figured out!"

I would have liked to explain to the person that I had been exposed to Walter Martin's views on Mormonism long before he had discovered Martin's writings, but my critic made it clear that the conversation was over. Even more, though, I would have liked to tell him that in wanting to be sure that I understand what another person is really saying, I was actually following some good counsel that I learned from Walter Martin himself.

The counsel came when I was a college student. At the time, Donald Grey Barnhouse was a well-known evangelical leader. The pastor for over three decades of the historic Tenth Presbyterian Church in Philadelphia, Barnhouse was also a national radio teacher ("The Bible Study Hour") and the editor of *Eternity* magazine. Several months after Barnhouse died in 1960, *Eternity* devoted a whole issue to his life and ministry, with several evangelical leaders testifying to Dr. Barnhouse's personal influence. One of the leaders who wrote was Walter Martin, whose tribute left a permanent impression on me.

Martin told of a time when he had been asked to lead a theological discussion, at a staff retreat held at Barnhouse's farm in rural Pennsylvania, on the topic of apologetics. During a lengthy break, Barnhouse and Martin strolled the grounds. On the walk Barnhouse carried a shotgun, which he used to shoot at scavenger birds, like crows and grackles, who bothered his favorites, the bluebirds. At one point Barnhouse interrupted the conversation to fell a bird in the distance. When he saw that he had hit his target he exclaimed, "That's one grackle less to bother my bluebirds."

When the two of them got closer to the fallen bird, however, Barnhouse saw that he had actually killed a bluebird. He was obviously distraught, but after a few minutes he observed to Martin that there was a spiritual lesson in what had just happened. He had been searching for a way, Barnhouse said, of warning Martin about jumping too quickly to the conclusion that a person is an enemy of the gospel, and now he had found a way to illustrate his concern. "You are right in defending the faith against its enemies, but you are too inclined to 'shoot from the hip' even as I was when I fired at this bird. In the excitement of the moment, it looked like a grackle; but a closer examination would have saved its life and my feelings. It is not wrong to contend for the gospel, but it is wrong to shoot first and ask questions later. What you think might be a grackle, an apostate, or an anti-Christ might well be a bluebird you looked at in a hurry."

Then Barnhouse placed his hand on Martin's shoulder and added: "Never forget this. Better to pass up an occasional grackle in theology and leave him with the Lord, than to shoot a bluebird and have to answer for it at the Judgment Seat of Christ."

He hadn't forgotten the wisdom of Barnhouse's counsel, Martin testified. And neither have I. Yes, we must contend for the truth against all those who oppose the gospel. But that means that we must be rigorous in making sure that we've discerned the truth about those against whom we contend. It may be that in thinking we're going after grackles, we end up killing bluebirds.

A Calvinist Option?

—◦◦◦—

I don't remember when I first came across a reference to O. Kendall White's book *Mormon Neo-Orthodoxy*, but I know it wasn't long after the book was published in 1987. The title intrigued me. Something "neo-" happening in Mormonism? If there *was* something new going on in Mormon theology, I wanted to know about it. So I ordered the book, and once I started reading it I couldn't put it down.

Professor White is a Mormon sociologist who is worried that Mormonism is drifting away from what he sees as the essentials of Joseph Smith's teachings. Here's what kept me turning the pages. Right at the beginning of his book White complains that some Mormons these days are starting to sound too much like Calvinists!

The reason that's a bad thing, White says, is that Joseph Smith established a religion that stands in stark opposition to the basic teachings of the Protestant Reformation. The Reformers of the sixteenth century — and the Calvinists were especially straightforward about this — taught these three themes: that God is sovereign and is totally "other" than the creation; that human beings are depraved sinners who are desperately in need of rescue by God; and that salvation is by grace alone. These three themes, says White, are profoundly different from Joseph Smith's insistence that the deity is finite; that human beings are capable of self-improvement; and that human beings can merit salvation by performing good works.[1]

Professor White may have been lamenting tendencies in what some Mormons are teaching these days, but as an enthusiastic Calvinist I was pleased to read what he had to say. I believe that God is sovereign, the one eternal God, unchanging in his being. I believe that God created us for fellowship with him; one of my favorite Calvinist formulations, from the Westminster Shorter Catechism, is that our "chief end" as human creatures "is to glorify God and to enjoy him forever." But we are fallen creatures — and desperately fallen. We have gotten into such a mess because of our rebellion against God that we can't do anything on our own to get out of it. If God doesn't do something to rescue us, we're hopelessly lost.

The wonderful message of the Bible, though, is that God has sent a Savior to do for us what we could never do for ourselves. The eternal Son of God, the Second Person of the Trinity, entered into our broken world and lived a life of perfect obedience to the demands of a righteous God. Because of Christ's obedience, he was able to bear our sins in his own body on the Cross of Calvary, shedding his blood to pay the ransom that delivers us — all who by grace are enabled to call out to God for salvation — from the ravages of our sinful condition.

1. O. Kendall White Jr., *Mormon Neo-Orthodoxy: A Crisis Theology* (Salt Lake City: Signature Books, 1987), xi-xviii.

I believe those things with all my heart. When someone wants to set forth the picture, then, of a finite God who encourages us to engage in a fundamental project of self-improvement in order to earn our salvation through the doing of good works, I cringe. Not only do I not like that kind of theology; I consider it very dangerous.

Why I'm Encouraged

So, when I read Professor White's complaint about some Mormons sounding too Calvinist these days, I was encouraged. And I was especially intrigued by his suggestion that Joseph Smith — in setting forth those teachings about a finite God, a self-perfectible human being, and salvation by works — was actually in tune with some of the emerging liberal theology in the Protestantism of his day. To be sure, says Professor White, Joseph Smith had a very different kind of religious perspective than the Protestant liberals. But, like them, he was seriously challenging the big themes of the Reformation about God's sovereignty, human depravity, and our desperate need for saving grace.

In the Protestant world, we do argue a lot with each other — traditionalists versus those who are more liberal — about the basic things Professor White mentions. It was fascinating to me to find out that these very same things might be an agenda that's being debated within the Mormon community.

And when I read the examples that Professor White offered of the things he's worried about in Mormonism, I could see why he was disturbed — and why I had reasons to be encouraged. Here, for example, is a comment quoted by White, by

Glenn L. Pearson, a longtime faculty member at Brigham Young University and the author of many widely read books in the Mormon community. Pearson is describing what it means to enter into God's presence with the proper spirit:

> There has to be down payment of a broken heart and a contrite spirit. Who has a broken heart and contrite spirit? One who is stripped of pride and selfishness. One who has come down in the depths of humility and prostrated himself before the Lord in mighty prayer and supplication. He has realized the awful guilt of his sins and has pled for the blood of Christ to be a covering to shield himself from the face of a just God. Such a one has made the down payment.[2]

That paragraph certainly strikes me as a solid biblical call for sinful people to plead for mercy from a righteous God. Suppose in a sermon in an evangelical church I said: "Glenn Pearson put it so well when he wrote that the kind of person God welcomes into his presence is one who 'has realized the awful guilt of his sins and pled for the blood of Christ." No one would question my orthodoxy or try to strip me of my evangelical credentials — unless, of course, they knew I was quoting a Mormon. But even then, what fault could they find in what Glenn Pearson actually says in that paragraph?

2. Glenn L. Pearson, *Know Your Religion* (Salt Lake City: Bookcraft, 1961), 169.

But Do They Mean the Same Thing?

Of course, this raises the big question that evangelicals always want to ask in a case like this. But does the Mormon writer really mean what *we* mean when we use those words? Is the God he's talking about the same God we worship? Is the Jesus he claims to be looking to for salvation the same Jesus we read about in the New Testament? Mormons may use the same words we use, but don't they mean something very different?

I'm going to explore these questions at a little more length soon. But here I want simply to make a basic point. If Glenn Pearson, in saying Calvinist-type things, is really using words in deceptive ways, why is Professor White so concerned about what Pearson says? White is convinced that there's an important theological issue at stake here. He sees a growing divide within the Mormon community on how Mormons understand the issues of sin and salvation. Either, he says, Mormons believe that God is sovereign, that human beings are guilty sinners, and that salvation is by grace alone, or — *or* — they believe that we have a finite God, we're self-perfectible humans, and salvation comes by doing good works.

That's the choice Professor White poses, and he sees the choice as an urgent one. If he's right about that, then we evangelicals will want to listen in to that debate very carefully. And if given the chance, we should be ready to join in the discussion — which is exactly what has been happening in recent decades. Those of us who have been present when Mormons argue with each other about various aspects of their belief system have seen all of this as a very encouraging sign. They haven't just been putting on a show for us. We can't simply dismiss all of these conversations as just one more way "the cults" are trying to deceive us.

In fact, even the label "cult" seems inappropriate for describing the Mormonism that we've seen up close. Jehovah's Witnesses — they're a cult. They stick to a party line. You don't find them arguing among themselves — at least in a way the rest of us can see and hear. If someone does insist on raising questions from within about Jehovah's Witness teachings, they're quickly expelled from the group. And the very idea of a world-class Jehovah's Witness university is a hard one to entertain.

Mormonism is a different story altogether. Brigham Young University is world class. It has an excellent faculty, with doctorates from some of the best graduate programs in the world. Some devout Mormons are well-known scholars at major secular schools. That's not the way a cult operates. The preferred label these days by those non-Mormons who have studied Mormonism carefully is "new religious movement." Indeed, Mormonism is one of the fastest-growing religious movements in the world. It deserves to be taken seriously by those of us who believe that what a person believes about God and salvation — and most of all, about the person and work of Jesus Christ — is important. Indeed, these are matters of eternal importance.

Getting at the Basics

———— *so so so* ————

I won't say his name here, but I will say that he's one of the evangelicals associated with the Religious Right. He and I disagree about a number of issues having to do with Christian political involvement. He even said once in public that Fuller Seminary, where I now serve as president, had "gone liberal." But when we ended up at the same conference sometime around the mid-1980s, we were able to have some friendly conversations.

We got into the topic of cooperating with people beyond the evangelical community on matters of common concern in public life, and he brought up the Mormons. He had cooperated with them on a number of issues, he said, and he always found them open to working together. Actually, he said, he really liked spending time with Mormon leaders. Then he said something that really surprised me: "I even think some of them are born again, in spite of some of the strange things they believe."

He was certainly right about the "strange things." There are teachings in Mormonism that I find strange indeed. And I'm

31

willing to argue about those specific things. Indeed, we evangelicals *have* argued about them — at great length! — in our meetings with our Mormon friends.

This is a good point at which to say something about how I view the motives of the Mormons with whom we've been having dialogues. Are they trying to convert us? That's what some evangelicals have claimed, and they've added that it seems to be working! I've heard it said that we — and I in particular — have become "soft on Mormonism."

Well, I'll repeat it again: I disagree with Mormon teachings on some very basic points. Joseph Smith reported that the Lord had told him that the creeds of the traditional churches — creeds whose teachings I hold as precious — were an "abomination" in the sight of God. That disturbs me deeply. I don't believe that Joseph Smith was a specially anointed prophet of God. I don't believe that the Book of Mormon is a new divine revelation. And so on.

Other critics have said that people like me are "being used" by the Mormons. The LDS church is looking for credibility, these folks say. Mormons want to be considered as a legitimate expression of Christianity. Encouraging dialogue with a select group of evangelicals is a part of an overall strategy to change their image.

All I have to go on in judging the motives of Mormons is what I discern in my Mormon friends after a decade of meeting with them on a regular basis. At the very beginning of our dialogues, they expressed their intentions in this way: during the hundred and seventy-some years since the founding of the LDS church, Mormonism has not been in close communication with representatives of historic Christianity — to put it mildly. There have been many angry denunciations back and forth, but no sustained attempts at trying to understand each other by actually talking to each other in calm tones. "This means," as one of them put it, "that we're not always sure we're even using the right language in telling you what we believe. Help us clarify what we want to say, so that at least we're not confusing things by talking past each other theologically." And that's what we've been doing together — making sure we've communicated accurately what we do and do not believe.

In the hundreds of hours I've spent with my Mormon dialogue partners, I've never detected any other motive than the desire to clarify what they're meaning to say in their theological formulations. To be sure, other things have emerged out of those dialogues. I was deeply moved when, recovering from serious surgery, I learned that my Mormon friends had been praying for my health. I've been moved, too, when they've asked their evangelical friends to pray for them in times of personal difficulty.

Christians After All?

So, does that mean that I'm saying — in spite of my declarations about how much I disagree with basic Mormon teachings — that they really are Christians after all? Let me explain as best I can how I see that question.

As I've been writing this book, the journal *First Things* has been featuring a running discussion between Mormons and others about the differences between LDS doctrines and traditional Christian teachings. Gerald McDermott is an evangelical scholar who helped get the discussion going in an exchange with Bruce Porter, a Harvard-trained Mormon scholar who serves the LDS church as a member of the First Quorum of the Seventy. McDermott, who has been engaging in a careful study of Mormon teaching, has drawn criticism from the LDS side for his insistence that "Mormonism as it stands cannot be successfully grafted" as yet another branch of the Christian tree. Mormon teaching on key doctrines is, he argues, nothing less than a refusal to accept "historic Christian orthodoxy." Significantly, though, McDermott goes on to say that in making the point about the rejection of orthodoxy, "I was not denying any relation between Mormonism and Christianity, and I was not talking about whether Mormons can be saved, which is a different matter."[1]

I agree with McDermott. But what does it mean to say that the state of one's eternal soul is "a different matter" than what one sets forth in one's theology? Here are two examples from the past that I find helpful.

Charles Hodge was a professor in the nineteenth century at Princeton Theological Seminary who was well known as a champion of Calvinist orthodoxy — and as an especially severe critic of the more liberal theology that was becoming increasingly influential in his day. One of the scholars with whom Hodge had very serious disagreements was the great German theologian Friedrich Schleiermacher. Hodge had studied theology in Germany in his younger years and had seen firsthand Schleiermacher's impact on the theological world. Most serious, in Hodge's opinion, was the German theologian's rejection of the Bible as an infallible divine revelation. Schleiermacher's

---

1. The original exchange between McDermott and Porter was "Is Mormonism Christian?" *First Things* (October 2008); the comments quoted here from McDermott are from "Correspondence," *First Things* (February 2009): 9.

embrace of the rationalist critique of biblical authority, Hodge insisted, had the effect of undermining the most fundamental tenets of the historic Christian faith.

Hodge's most enduring published work is found in his *Systematic Theology,* which he wrote several decades after Schleiermacher's death. In those pages he sets forth his objections to Schleiermacher's theology, pulling no punches about the dangers of the German theologian's views. At the same time, though, Hodge offers a brief personal comment about Schleiermacher in a footnote. During his studies in Germany, Hodge reports, he had frequently attended services at Schleiermacher's church, and he had been impressed by the fact that the hymns sung in those services "were always evangelical and spiritual in an eminent degree, filled with praise and gratitude to our Redeemer." He goes on to note that he had been told by one of Schleiermacher's colleagues that often in the evenings the theologian would call his family together, saying: "Hush, children; let us sing a hymn of praise to Christ." And then Hodge adds this tribute to Schleiermacher: "Can we doubt that he is singing those praises now? To whomever Christ is God, St. John assures us, Christ is a Saviour."[2]

In paying this tribute to Schleiermacher, Hodge isn't watering down his theological critique. He has made it very clear that Schleiermacher's theology undercuts the historic belief in Christ's full divinity. Yet he also allows that Schleiermacher's personal faith in Christ was real — even if it was not supported by the teachings about Christ that Hodge set forth in his theology.

---

2. Charles Hodge, *Systematic Theology,* vol. 2 (Peabody, MA: Hendrickson Publishers, 2003), 440, n. 1.

Another example, also from the nineteenth century. Charles Haddon Spurgeon is one of my heroes. I own a twenty-volume set of his sermons, and I frequently read and reread them. Often called "the Prince of Preachers," Spurgeon was a gifted proclaimer of the gospel through whose ministry many people came to a saving faith in Christ. Like Hodge, he was a champion of Calvinist orthodoxy, and at the heart of his message was the insistence that salvation comes by sovereign grace alone, through the merits of Jesus Christ, who went to the Cross to do for us what we could never do for ourselves. In his sermons, Spurgeon often particularly criticizes Roman Catholicism for what he saw as a heavy reliance on "good works" as a means of earning salvation.

In 1860 Spurgeon and his wife visited Belgium, and in reporting on his trip he offers an account of their visit to a Catholic congregation in that country. Here is his description of what he experienced while attending that worship service:

> In Brussels, I heard a good sermon in a Romish church. The place was crowded with people, many of them standing, though they might have had a seat for a halfpenny or a farthing; and I stood, too; and the good priest — for I believe he is a good man — preached the Lord Jesus with all his might. He spoke of the love of Christ, so that I, a very poor hand at the French language, could fully understand him, and my heart kept beating within me as he told of the beauties of Christ, and of the preciousness of His blood, and of His power to save the chief of sinners. He did not say, "justification by faith," but he did say, "efficacy of the blood," which comes to very much the same thing. He did not tell us that we were saved by grace, and not by our

works; but he did say that all the works of men were less than nothing when brought into competition with the blood of Christ, and that the blood of Jesus alone could save. True, there were objectionable sentences, as naturally there must be in a discourse delivered under such circumstances; but I could have gone to the preacher, and have said to him, "Brother, you have spoken the truth"; and if I had been handling the text, I must have treated it in the same way that he did, if I could have done it as well. I was pleased to find my own opinion verified, in his case, that there are, even in the apostate church, some who cleave unto the Lord, — some sparks of Heavenly fire that flicker amidst the rubbish of old superstition, some lights that are not blown out, even by the strong wind of Popery, but still cast a feeble gleam across the waters sufficient to guide the soul to the rock Christ Jesus.[3]

Back to Gerald McDermott's comment that there is a difference between lodging serious criticisms of a person's theology and claiming that the person is not destined for heaven. Both Hodge and Spurgeon were making the same point. Hodge thought that Schleiermacher's theology seriously undercut the historic Christian faith — but he was confident that Schleiermacher had gone to heaven. Spurgeon regularly criticized the Catholic thought and practice of his day as focusing on something other than the atoning work of Jesus Christ for salvation — but he credited a Catholic priest with pointing his congregation to "the rock Christ Jesus."

3. Quoted in Lewis Drummond, *Spurgeon: Prince of Preachers* (Grand Rapids: Kregel, 1992), 343-44.

"Do You Think I'm a Christian?"

My assistant came into my office to tell me that a caller wanted to talk with me: "He says he's a Mormon and he wants to ask you a question about his personal faith. Should I tell him you're too busy?" Then she quickly added: "He seems quite nice, and he says he isn't calling to argue with you about anything."

I decided to take the call. The person on the line asked whether he could briefly tell me about his spiritual journey. I wasn't sure I wanted to hear his story, but my assistant was right: he did seem quite nice.

He had been raised in a mainline Protestant church, he told me, and during his youth he had never felt challenged to make any serious commitment to Christianity. As a student at a university — one of the most distinguished ones academically — his roommate for all four years was a Mormon. "He was very bright, and very committed to his faith," the caller reported. "It was the first time I encountered someone who was serious about his religious convictions and who was also interesting to argue with." In his senior year my caller himself joined the Latter-day Saints. "That was ten years ago," he said. "Lately, though, I've had some questions. I've read about your dialogue with some of our LDS scholars, and I'd like you to tell me whether you think I'm a Christian."

I told him that I'd have to ask him some questions, and I'd need some honest answers from him. He agreed. Here's the gist of our exchange:

"How many gods are there?" I asked.

"Well, there is one Godhead, made up of three divine Persons — Father, Son, and Holy Spirit," he responded.

"Will you ever become a god like them?"

"Oh no. I hope I'm becoming more Christ-like, but only the three Persons of Godhead are worthy of worship. More *like* God — yes. To *be* a god — no way!"

"What is the basis for your salvation? Do you earn it by your good works?"

"No, my good works can't save me. I'm saved by grace, through the atoning work of Christ on the Cross. My good works — those I perform in gratitude to what He has done for me."

I gave him my assessment. "I can't judge your heart, but I can say something about your answers to my questions. If someone else had called me out of the blue, telling me that he was a Methodist or a Presbyterian, and asked me whether I thought he was a true Christian, and if he had given those same answers that you've given, I would say, 'Yes, those are good Christian answers.' So, I have to say to you that I think you've answered some important questions in a very Christian way."

He then pushed me a step further. "Well, I really do believe what I said to you. So — do you think I should leave Mormonism if that is what I believe?" I paused before answering. Then I told him I'd recommend that he stay in the LDS church. "But keep saying those things," I urged. "And if the Mormon leaders ever tell you that you can't give those answers to the basic questions, then I'd recommend that you leave Mormonism."

That happened three days before I went to Nauvoo, Illinois. I'd been thinking a lot about my visit to Nauvoo just before the young man called. Our Mormon-evangelical dialogue group had decided to hold our meeting this time around at Nauvoo, the town where the Mormons had settled in 1839, after escaping from their persecutors in Missouri, and from which they would flee once more in 1846, two and a half years after Joseph Smith was murdered in the nearby Carthage jail.

Robert Millet, my Mormon friend from Brigham Young University, and I were scheduled to give talks to the group on our last evening in Nauvoo — from the podium in the Seventies Hall, where Joseph Smith had lectured regularly to Mormons who were being sent out on missionary journeys. Each of us was going to describe what we'd been learning from our dialogues and to say some things about where we hoped the dialogues were going. As the time approached I struggled with what I should say. Then that phone call came. After the exchange with the young man, I knew what I would tell my Mormon friends.

In my Nauvoo talk I reported the phone conversation, and I formulated my thoughts about the future around the young man's story. I told the group that our dialogues had given me the hope that there would come a day when all of us could say together what that young man had said in response to my questions. God is God, and we are not. The Godhead alone — Father, Son, and Holy Spirit — is worthy of worship. Salvation comes by grace alone, through the substitutionary atoning work of Christ on Calvary. Our good works cannot contribute to our salvation — they are done in response to a grace that has accomplished for us what we could never accomplish for ourselves.

Several of the Mormons in the group told me that they could already give those answers. I believed them and was encouraged.

Duped?

Again, there are many evangelicals who are convinced that those of us on the evangelical side who are involved in these dialogues have been duped by the Mormons. Worse than that, they're convinced that by engaging in friendly — and hopeful — dialogue with representatives of Mormonism, we're hurting the cause of the gospel.

Just before I started writing this book I Googled the combination of "Mouw" and "Mormon," and I came up with over 9,000 hits. You only have to glance quickly at the headlines of the first fifty or so to get the picture. Promoting the idea of friendly dialogue with Mormons isn't a popular thing to do in the evangelical world. And you really get into trouble if you suggest that we evangelicals haven't always been fair in our portrayals of what Mormons believe.

I certainly don't want to be duped by Mormons. But I have a good reason for thinking that this is not what's happening. The test for me is not what Mormons say to me, but what they say to each other. And I've paid considerable attention to what's being said about important spiritual and theological matters *within* Mormonism. Some of what I hear and see I find troubling. But more often than not I find things that encourage me.

I've heard Mormon leaders preach sermons to their fellow members about the importance of recognizing our sinfulness and of the need to look to God's grace as the only hope for salvation. And I've heard them speak movingly about the atoning work that Jesus accomplished on our behalf on the Cross of Calvary.

A student of mine at Fuller Seminary did all of her undergraduate studies at Brigham Young University. As an evangelical studying at a Mormon school, she told me, she was treated with respect and sensitivity by her professors. I asked her whether the kinds of things we're hearing these days from Mormons in our dialogues are different from what many of those same scholars are teaching Mormon students in their classrooms. She smiled: "No, you're getting the real thing from them. There were times when I, as the evangelical in the class, was more comfortable with what the Mormon professor was saying than my fellow students!" I took that as an important word of encouragement.

Pushback Questions

—⁓⟩⟨⟩⟨⟩⁓—

I know that what I've been saying here will leave many nagging questions, even with folks who aren't hostile to the project I'm describing. My main concern in what I've been saying thus far is to invite us to nurture friendlier relations with the Mormon community. I want us to listen carefully to our Mormon neighbors, without deciding ahead of time what they "really" believe. Patience, humility, a willingness to admit our own shortcomings — all of these are necessary to move the dialogue forward.

But I'm not suggesting that by forming more positive relations all of our differences will magically melt away. That certainly isn't what has happened to me. I still struggle with some big questions about Mormon thought. I want to go into a little more detail here on three of those big questions.

The biggest question has to do with Jesus. When it comes right down to it, are Mormons talking about the same Jesus in whom we traditional Christians are putting our trust?

Another big question has to do with the authority of the Bible. Mormons accept the whole Bible as containing God's re-vealed will for us. They typically use the word "infallible" in talking about the Bible's authority as the Word of God. But then they add these other books: the Book of Mormon, the Doctrine and Covenants, the Pearl of Great Price. And they see these other writings as on a par with the Bible. Isn't that enough simply to vote them off the Christian island?

And then there's Mormonism's founder. Joseph Smith started the whole thing with the announcement that he had received new revelations from God. And furthermore, he in-sisted that there were more revelations to come, and they would be transmitted to the rest of the human race through the office of prophet — to which he had been appointed by God. What are we to make of all that?

I care deeply about these topics, and they've loomed large in my own conversations with Mormon scholars and church leaders. The issues at stake are of major importance. I con-tinue to struggle with the questions as I work at my own rela-tionships with the Mormon community.

Since this is an ongoing struggle for me, I make no pretence of being able to offer definitive answers here. But I do know that I owe my fellow Christians at least some further thoughts on matters of such great importance. So the next three chap-ters deal with each of these three topics. Dealing with them will require a little more theological detail than I've offered thus far. For those who might not want that much detail, I hope they'll at least try to pick up the main points.

The Same Jesus?

———◦◦◦———

At a large gathering of scholars of religion several years ago, I ran into a Protestant theologian who is well known for his very liberal reinterpretations of traditional Christian ideas. In spite of our rather deep disagreements on matters of faith, we are on friendly terms. On this occasion we agreed to meet later that evening for a leisurely dinner together. Our conversation at the meal was a stimulating one. We launched quickly into serious theological discussion, and by the end he made it clear that while he liked and respected me personally, he found my views about Jesus Christ to be deeply offensive. I was insisting that Jesus is the eternal Son of God who was sent from heaven to do for us what we could never do for ourselves: Jesus offered himself up to the Father as a perfect sacrifice for our sins. This means, I argued, that no human being can hope to achieve salvation apart from the atoning work of Jesus Christ.

My theologian friend was adamant in his endorsement of religious pluralism. As someone raised and educated in the

Christian tradition, he said, he could admit to a special personal "connection" to Jesus of Nazareth. But he was, to use his own word, "outraged" by my insistence that Jesus is a unique Savior. God is larger than any one religion's definitions, he argued, and all of us need to be celebrating the fact that there are many different paths to salvation.

My friend was in a bit of a grumpy mood as we left the restaurant to walk back to our hotel, and I was eager to lighten things up a bit. As we walked along a side street I noticed that someone had scrawled these words on a telephone pole: "Trust Jesus!" I put my arm around my companion's shoulder and directed his attention to the words. "Hey, my friend," I said in a teasing voice, "I think the Lord is trying to send you a message." He quickly retorted in irritated tones: "I'm not afraid to trust Jesus! But not *your* Jesus! Not *your* Jesus!"

I confess that in many lengthy discussions about Jesus with Mormon scholars over the past several years, I'm the one who has been tempted to say accusingly, "Not *your* Jesus! Not *your* Jesus!" I came into those discussions knowing full well, I thought, what the Latter-day Saints believe about Jesus, and I wasn't eager to have them try to convince me that I was operating with preconceived notions that were mistaken.

I still have some serious misgivings, but the misgivings do not run quite as deep as they did earlier.

In our evangelical-Mormon dialogues we've talked at length about many important theological topics. But none is more important than the question about Jesus. What a person believes about Jesus Christ is not only a central issue for theological discussion; it is an issue that has eternal significance for all human beings. The jailer in Acts 16 addressed the fundamental question directly to Paul and Silas: "Sirs, what must I do to be saved?" And their answer was equally direct: "Believe on the Lord Jesus, and you will be saved." Our theological discussions about the person and work of Christ aren't merely academic excursions. They get at the most basic issue that any human being can confront: How do we get right with God?

Reasons for Hope

In my discussions with my Mormon friends about Jesus, there are at least three things that have made me hopeful that we can make some progress together in our continuing discussions.

One encouraging factor is that we've been making some headway in developing a shared understanding of some basic theological terms. In his groundbreaking book-length dialogue with evangelical theologian Craig Blomberg, the LDS scholar Stephen Robinson made the important observation that "LDS terminology often seems naive, imprecise and even sometimes sloppy by Evangelical standards." But traditional Christians, Robinson observed, "have had centuries in which to polish and refine their terminology" — and besides, he added, "we have no professional clergy to keep our theological language finely tuned."[1]

Given that situation, we should at least work to be sure we're understanding each other better. And that has been happening.

A second reason for hope is my personal realization that

---

1. Craig L. Blomberg and Stephen E. Robinson, *How Wide the Divide? A Mormon and an Evangelical in Conversation* (Downers Grove: InterVarsity Press, 1997), 156.

many — not all, but many — of the arguments that I as a Calvinist evangelical have with Mormons are not too far removed from the arguments that I've had with theologians who represent traditions that are clearly in the Christian mainstream. We evangelicals argue at length with Roman Catholics about whether the Bible is our only authority, or whether there are additional sources of revealed truth that must be taken as equally authoritative with the Old and New Testaments. The question of "divinization" — of how we must think about the apostle John's promise that, while we are already God's children, "it does not yet appear what we shall be," but we can be assured that someday "we will be like him" — has been much discussed between Christians of the Western churches and the Eastern Orthodox. And the Mormon insistence that the "good work" that we must perform in connection with placing our faith in Christ — well, this is not unlike a claim that I regularly argue about with my friends in the Arminian tradition.

Of course, in the end, we might decide that our arguments as traditional Christians with Mormons are very different in kind than the sorts of arguments we carry on among ourselves within the mainstream Christian tradition. But the recognition that something like these and other teachings have been long debated within mainstream Christianity can give us some new handles for assessing the unique ways in which Mormons talk about such matters.

A third hopeful sign is the kind of interpretations that my Mormon friends offer for what many of us have taken to be very harsh-sounding LDS claims. Not the least of these is the insistence by Joseph Smith that the "creeds" that many of us profess are an "abomination." I haven't stopped worrying about that kind of verdict from Mormonism's founder. But I'm also encouraged to see some serious Mormon wrestling with the issues, rather than a simple repetition of Joseph Smith's harsh rhetoric.

My Mormon friend Robert Millet wrote a book several years ago, explaining at length Mormon views about Jesus. The book, *A Different Jesus? The Christ of the Latter-day Saints,* was directed primarily to non-Mormons, and Millet took very seriously the kinds of questions traditional Christians have about Mormon theology. To provide a framework for his discussion, I agreed to write both a foreword and an afterword for the book, in the hopes of encouraging the ongoing dialogue.

In my comments about Millet's case, I made it clear that I have some strong objections to the Mormon understanding of Jesus, as he presents it in his book. At the same time, though, I was impressed by his careful reading of evangelical authors — John Stott, Cornelius Plantinga, and John McArthur, among others — who have clearly set forth the traditional Christian perspective on Christ's person and redemptive mission. In Millet's interactions with those theologians, I had the sense that, despite the fact that I had some serious disagreements with the case he was making, Millet was at least focusing on the same Jesus whom I accept as the heaven-sent Savior. Like Charles Hodge and Charles Spurgeon, I do believe that people can have a defective theology about Christ while still putting their trust in the true Christ.

I've taken much heat from a number of evangelicals for offering that positive assessment of the Mormon perspective as Millet sets it forth. I stick to what I said about his views, but I also acknowledge that the critics are right to keep pushing me and others on this. We evangelicals are rightly nervous

about anything that looks like a departure from the key elements of what we see as the biblical portrayal of who Jesus
Christ is.

The Creeds an "Abomination"?

Like most other evangelical theologians, I look to the history of
Christian thought for guidance about how best to understand
the biblical Jesus. Early on, the church saw the need to summa-
rize what the believing community insisted upon as the non-
negotiable teachings of the Bible. This took the form of the
Apostles' Creed. But in subsequent centuries, even that combination — the Bible plus the Apostles' Creed — was not enough.
Some people began to teach views that departed from the way
the church has understood the biblical message, especially
about the person and work of Jesus Christ. So some additional
creedal statements were adopted, chief among them being the
Nicene Creed.

I take the teachings of the Apostles' Creed and the Nicene
Creed with utmost seriousness. I look to them for my understanding of biblical orthodoxy. When people question the content of those creeds, I begin to worry about whether they really
understand the Christian faith.

So, like any other evangelical, I bristle at some of the things
said about traditional Christian teachings by early Mormon
leaders. And one of the most shocking of those statements is
Joseph Smith's claim that God had told him that all of the
Christian tradition's "creeds were an abomination."[2]

2. Joseph Smith Jr., *History of the Church of Jesus Christ of Latter-day*

That certainly struck me as a deal breaker when I first came across it. My two favorite creeds — Apostles' and Nicene — an abomination in the sight of God? Surely once that gets put on the table there's nothing more to talk about.

But my Mormon friends have encouraged me to stick with the conversation. They've done some homework on how to portray that seemingly harsh statement in a less offensive light.

It helps to put the Mormon view of creeds into a larger historical context. There are some people, people most of us would consider to be clearly within the Christian camp, who also take a decidedly negative view of the historic creeds. Historians of American religion depict Mormonism as one of several "Restorationist" movements that emerged in the eighteenth and nineteenth centuries. The "Stone-Campbell" churches — the Christian Church (Disciples of Christ), the Churches of Christ, and the Christian Churches — are also known for their "No creed but Christ" manifesto, but they do hold to what most evangelicals would consider to be the essentials of biblical orthodoxy: the Trinity, the full divinity of Christ, salvation by the atoning work of the Cross, the supreme authority of the Bible. What those Christians object to in the creeds is not necessarily the content, but the ways in which the creedal documents sometimes (they would say frequently) come to function as having an authority that rivals that of the New Testament.

And this is how some Mormon scholars interpret Joseph Smith's blunt rejection of the creeds. One Mormon scholar, John Welch, observes that there's nothing in the content of the

---

Saints, ed. B. H. Roberts (Salt Lake City: The Church of Jesus Christ of Latter-day Saints, 1950), 1:18-19.

Apostles' Creed that a Mormon would simply reject. The content is fine. The problem is in the way that innocent-sounding creed set a precedent for more creedal documents to follow. In the course of Christian history, "the liberty of the pure and simple spirit that had prevailed in the apostolic era" began to give way to a doctrinal "absolutism" that imposed too many rigid definitions on people who simply wanted to follow Jesus.[3]

The Nicene Creed

The Nicene Creed seems especially offensive to Mormons in this regard. The late Gordon Hinckley, speaking as the LDS church's leading Prophet, put it this way: "We do not accept the Nicene Creed, nor any other creed based on tradition and the conclusions of men."[4] In his dialogue with Craig Blomberg, Stephen Robinson elaborated on that kind of objection by depicting the authors of the Nicene Creed as introducing Greek philosophical concepts into Christian thought, thus imposing alien categories onto the message of the Bible. This anti-"Greek" theme comes up often in Mormon discussions, with the insistence, in Robinson's words, that Mormons simply "reject the interpretive straitjacket imposed on the Bible by the Hellenized

3. John W. Welch, "'All Their Creeds Were an Abomination': A Brief Look at the Creeds as Part of the Apostasy," in *Prelude to the Restoration: From Apostasy to the Restored Church* (Provo, UT, and Salt Lake City: Religious Studies Center, Brigham Young University and Deseret Book, 2004), 228–49. Also on-line at http://rsc.byu.edu/archived/prelude-restoration-apostasy-restored-church/14-%E2%80%9Call-their-creeds-were-abomination%E2%80%9D-brief-l.

4. Gordon B. Hinckley, "What Are People Asking about Us?" at http://lds.org.ensign/1998/11/what-are-people-asking-about-us?lang=eng.

church." For Mormons, Robinson argued, "disagreeing with the Councils of Nicaea and Chalcedon is not the same as disagreeing with the New Testament." Mormon teaching "does contradict Plato," he says, but that doesn't make it unbiblical.[5]

Those of us who adhere to the Christian tradition have an obvious answer to this. The great Jesuit theologian John Courtney Murray put it well in response to people who see a lot of "Greek" ideas in the traditional creeds. When the experts who gathered at Nicaea introduced the ideas of "being" into their formulations about Christ, that the Son is *homoousia* — "of *one being/substance*" — with God the Father, they weren't borrowing an idea from Greek philosophy; they were reaching for words that would capture the sense of Scripture, in order to guard against dangerous misreadings of the biblical texts.[6] Murray's insistence that such formulations are not only good but inevitable is confirmed in subsequent Protestant history as well. Even the strictest "no creed but Christ" churches introduce, in some form or another, extra-biblical formulations that rule out eccentric interpretations of biblical teachings.

Indeed, it's on this very point that many of us will want to push our Mormon friends about their own elaborate collection of extra-biblical documents that elaborate on — and add much to — the content of the Old and New Testaments. But here I want to stick to their perspective on the classic Christian creeds.

On one reading of the central assertions of the Nicene Creed, Mormons should have no problem in providing their endorsement. They, too, believe that the Father and the Son

5. Blomberg and Robinson, *How Wide the Divide?* 59-60, 79.

6. John Courtney Murray, *The Problem of God: Yesterday and Today* (New Haven: Yale University Press, 1964), 53-57.

are "of one being." Indeed, if we take that claim in isolation from everything else in the creed, it actually comports quite nicely with Mormon Christology. After all, Mormons are famous for having taught that the members of the Godhead and human beings are "of the same species."[7] This means, then, that not only are the Father and the Son "of the same substance," but they share that metaphysical character with all human beings.

And that's exactly where the problem comes up between Mormons and the rest of us. And it's a problem that cuts deep. Judaism and Christianity have been united in their insistence that the Creator and the creation — including God's human creatures — are divided by an unbridgeable "being" gap. God is the *totaliter aliter,* the "Wholly Other," who is in a realm of existence that's radically distinct from the creation that the triune God called into existence out of nothing *(ex nihilo)* by a sovereign decree ("Let there be . . . and there was . . .").

On this view of things, to confuse the Creator's being with anything in his creation violates a fundamental biblical theme. The Mormon "same species" contention, on the other hand, sees the differences between God and humankind, not in terms of an unbridgeable gap of being, but as best expressed in the language of "more" and "less" — quantitative rather than qualitative differences.

So, does that leave us at an impasse, beyond which no significant dialogue is possible about the person and work of Christ? I think not. I want to point to two potentially productive areas of theological focus for pursuing the conversation:

7. See, for example, "Discourse by Elder O. F. Whitney," *The Latter-day Saints' Millennial Star* 57, no. 3 (January 17, 1895): 34.

soteriology, that is, the theology of salvation; and the historical development of doctrine. I will briefly explain here how the conversations in each of those areas might go.

Theology of Salvation

Mormonism is often portrayed as a self-deification program — and not without some legitimacy, given the popularity of the Lorenzo Snow couplet: "What Man now is, God once was; what God now is, Man may become." My Mormon friends are quick to point out, however, that this couplet has no official canonical status — indeed, Gordon Hinckley famously told *Time* magazine that he had no idea what it means to say "As God is, man may become." Hinckley's own formulations typically emphasized how Christ's Atonement allows us, in the power of the Holy Spirit, to acquire Christ-like characteristics.

And the fact is that there are strong elements in much of Mormon thought that are closely aligned with traditional Christian soteriology, with its insistence on a human sinfulness that requires nothing less than the atoning power of the heaven-sent Savior for our salvation. Here, for example, is Elder Jeffrey Holland, of the Quorum of the Twelve, describing Christ's redemptive mission:

[I]n a spiritual agony that began in Gethsemane and a physical payment that was consummated on the cross of Calvary, [Jesus] took upon himself every sin and sorrow, every heartache and infirmity, every sickness, sadness, trial, tribulation experienced by the children of God from Adam to the end of the world. How he did that is a stun-

ning mystery, but he did it . . . [making] merciful interces-
sion for all the children of men.[8]

Joseph Smith himself gave an orthodox-sounding account
of salvation matters, on the occasion of the founding of the
Church of Jesus Christ of Latter-day Saints in April of 1830:
"we know," he said, "that all men must repent and believe on
the name of Jesus Christ, and worship the Father in his name,
and endure in faith on his name to the end, or they cannot be
saved in the kingdom of God." And then he added: "And we
know that justification through the grace of our Lord and Savior Jesus Christ is just and true, and we know also that sancti-
fication through the grace of our Lord and Savior Jesus Christ
is just and true, to all those who love and serve God with all
their mights, minds, and strength" (Doctrines and Covenants
20:29-30).

In statements like these we find many classical Christian
soteriological expressions. Human beings are fallen and incapable of securing salvation by their own efforts. Only a Savior
sent from heaven could save us, and he did so in a redemptive
mission that culminated in the atoning sacrifice on the Cross
of Calvary.

We can also see in these statements that the more Mormons gravitate toward the language of classical soteriology
the more they also adopt ways of talking about God that echo
the classical tradition. It's significant, for example, that in that
same 1830 address Joseph Smith articulates a robust doctrine
of God: "[W]e know," he says, "that there is a God in heaven,

---

8. Jeffrey R. Holland, *Christ and the New Covenant* (Salt Lake City: Deseret
Book Company, 1997), 228.

who is infinite and eternal, from everlasting to everlasting the same unchangeable God, the framer of heaven and earth, and all things which are in them" (Doctrines and Covenants 20:17).

There's an important topic here, then, for continuing theological discussion. And that discussion will proceed best, as I see it, when we focus on the basic dilemmas of the human condition.

I get a lot of good theology from hymns. And some of the best theology in hymns can be found in Christmas carols. Here's one of my favorite hymn lines, from "O Little Town of Bethlehem": "The hopes and fears of all the years are met in Thee tonight." This points to an important topic for theological discussion between traditional Christians and Mormons. What are the basic desires and dilemmas of the human condition? What are the hopes and fears that Jesus came from heaven to address in his redemptive mission?

In my theology, at the heart of it all is the need for rescue from our sinful condition. We're lost sinners, rebels against God. And we're so enmeshed in our sinful rebellion that we can't get out of the mess by our own efforts. We need a Savior. And God has provided one in the person of Jesus Christ. "While we were yet sinners, Christ died for us" (Romans 5:8). Wonderful news!

When I talk about all of that with my Mormon friends, many of them — scholars and church leaders — agree. And I take their agreement as a wonderful sign. But for me the next question is, Given that we agree that we're sinners desperately in need of divine rescue, what kind of Savior would it take to save us? What does Jesus Christ need to be like in his own "being" in order to accomplish salvation for the likes of us?

And this is where it gets interesting. Is the gap between human unworthiness and divine mercy that seems to be implicit in so many of Mormonism's own formulations of the human predicament and the greatness of salvation — is that gap capable of being explained adequately by a theology in which the God who saves and the humans who receive that gracious salvation are "of the same species" ontologically?

Note that in posing these questions to my Mormon friends, I'm not meaning to question the sincerity of their professions of faith in the saving power of Jesus Christ. What I'm asking them is what I take it the Princeton theologian Charles Hodge would have wanted to ask of his liberal counterpart Friedrich Schleiermacher: Given your obviously sincere love of the Savior in whom you're trusting for your salvation, is the theology that you teach capable of *sustaining* that trust?

Developing Doctrine

Now, my second focus: the relationship between the classic creeds and the development of doctrine.

The reason why the Christian church of the fourth century had to say something about the "being" of Christ was that disagreements had arisen that simply had to be adjudicated if there was to be a clear and commonly accepted understanding of what it means for Jesus to be the One who "for us and for our salvation . . . came down from heaven," as the Nicene Creed puts it. And while the Latter-day Saints presently exempt themselves from that consensus — sticking with, as we saw John Welch putting it, "the pure and simple spirit that had prevailed in the apostolic era" — it will be interesting to see what happens when the LDS leadership decides that this "pure and simple spirit" is being violated in various Mormon expressions about the person and work of Christ.

My own prediction is that as the scholarly study of Mormon doctrine continues to grow in impressive ways, the need for new doctrinal decisions will become pressing. As Mormonism's younger generation becomes increasingly well educated and well versed in the various strands of religious thought in the larger culture, new challenges to standard Mormon teachings will inevitably emerge.

A case in point: as I was writing about these matters I read an issue of the "progressive" Mormon magazine, *Sunstone,* in which there was a report about a discussion group that had met in a Phoenix home on an evening in October 2009. The writer was himself a participant, and he described with some enthusiasm the range of views represented in the group, which he characterized as a gathering of "misfit Mormons." The intellectual "tent was certainly large that evening," he wrote: "Internet Mormons, Chapel Mormons, Ex-Mormons, Post Mormons, Feminist Mormons, Gay Mormons" — and even, he says, "a couple of Catholics thrown in to add some diversity."[9]

As a longtime subscriber to *Sunstone,* I could have recommended some of *Sunstone's* other writers to add yet more diversity to the mix: Jungian Mormons, Deconstructionist Mormons, Process Theology Mormons, Mormons who sneak off to Anglican services, and so on.

The very existence of an increasingly expanding Mormon intellectual "tent" is a relatively new phenomenon. It's not unthinkable that there may come a time when the LDS church is faced with the need to establish boundaries in how the faithful

9. John Wilcox, "Island of the Misfit Mormons," *Sunstone* (March 2010): 12.

are to understand — to make clear sense of — "the pure and simple spirit that had prevailed in the apostolic era." My hunch is that when that happens, it will be very much like a "Nicene moment" for Mormonism.

The possibility that such a moment may be coming is, as I see it, a good reason for some of us evangelicals to be around in the hope of being able to join in that conversation!

Of Books and Prophets

—⟨⟨⟨⟩⟩⟩—

In talking about the Mormon view of revelation and authority, one point needs to be made clear at the outset. It isn't just that the Mormons have more revealed books than the rest of us. They do, of course; but to say that doesn't get to the heart of the issue. The real point is that books are not where the true authority resides for Mormons.

Evangelical Christians often miss this basic point. We believe in *sola scriptura;* the "Bible alone" is our supreme authority on the fundamental issues of belief and practice. But in a sense, of course, that's a little misleading. Back in the 1970s, when evangelicals were passionately debating questions relating to "biblical inerrancy," James Packer — a theological giant in the evangelical community — gave what was for me a memorable address on biblical authority at a Wheaton College conference. He surprised no one by affirming his own strong support for the idea of biblical inerrancy. But then he went on to remind us all that holding to an inerrant Bible by itself doesn't guarantee orthodoxy. We must, Packer said, be clear about the fact that the Bible points us to God's supreme revelation in our Lord and Savior, Jesus Christ.

What has stuck in my mind is the way Professor Packer illustrated his point. He quoted from the hymn "Break Thou the Bread of Life": "Beyond the sacred page, I seek Thee, Lord." In our devotion to the authoritative written Word, Packer said, we must always allow it to point us to the worship and service of the Living Word.

For traditional Christianity, then, the Bible's supreme authority is a "pointing" authority. It points us beyond itself to Jesus Christ, who alone is "the way, the truth, and the life" (John 14:6). When we say that "the Bible alone" is our ultimate authority, we're insisting that in our efforts to comprehend God's will for us in Jesus Christ we need a lot of help in understanding the details, and that anything that contradicts what the Bible tells us about God's plan for the creation has to be ruled out of bounds. This doesn't mean that we can't learn from other sources — our intellectual pursuits, our personal experiences, the teachings that come to us from the Christian past — but when such deliverances conflict with what the Bible clearly says to us, the Bible trumps all other sources.

The Office of the Prophet

For Mormonism, this reliance on writings — sacred "pages" — is secondary. What they see as primary is the office of the prophet. The most important thing to Mormons about their early history isn't that Joseph Smith dug up the golden plates containing the Book of Mormon in the early decades of the nineteenth century. More importantly, Mormonism teaches that in the person of Joseph Smith the ancient office of prophet was restored.

Here's the first verse of a much-sung Mormon hymn, composed by W. W. Phelps for the dedication of the first Mormon temple, in Kirtland, Ohio, in 1836:

The Spirit of God like a fire is burning;
The latter-day glory begins to come forth;
The visions and blessings of old are returning;
The angels are coming to visit the earth.

For the followers of Joseph Smith, the religious movement that he had established was a restoring of something that had long been lost. And it wasn't just the finding of an ancient book along with the adding of some new books. It was the restoration of the kind of heavenly visitations that occurred in ancient times.

There were times in Old Testament history when godly people had no authoritative book to rely on in understanding the will of God. Noah, Abraham, Moses — none of these had anything like a Bible. God spoke directly to them. Similarly, in the New Testament and the early church, there was much reliance on oral tradition — the memories of what Jesus had taught and done, and later the memories of the teachings of the apostles.

There came a point, though, when these testimonies were written down; and eventually those writings that the church came to see as supremely authoritative became — in the forming of "the canon" — our Bible. Christians became a "people of the Book."

Mormons insist on going "behind" the process that produced "the Book." What matters about the Bible is that it contains the teachings that had come directly from God to apostles and prophets. And now, they argue, the prophetic office has been restored. This means that "the canon" isn't "closed." Revelations continue. What binds together the Bible, then, with the Book of Mormon, the Doctrines and Covenants, the Pearl of Great Price, and any new authoritative deliverances from the continuing line of the true prophets is that they receive their authority from the fact that they come to us from those who have occupied — and continue to occupy — the office of the prophet.

New Revelations

I was attending a meeting between several evangelical pastors and some LDS church leaders. After a lengthy discussion of the issues of authority and revelation, we paused to give our impressions of what had transpired. One of the evangelicals offered this assessment. He told the LDS participants how much he admired them, and how much he appreciated the friendliness and candor with which they had presented their views. "The very fact that I have such a positive view of you folks as individuals," he said, "makes it very difficult to tell you how grieved I am because of what you've been saying. You talk with such sincerity about Christ as the only Savior, and about his atoning work on Calvary. But I simply cannot take what you say about such things at face value. I believe that the Bible alone is our authority. Anyone who adds to the biblical message is openly rejecting what the Bible says about itself. The Christ that you're talking about cannot be the Jesus of the

Word of God. Your so-called Gospel is a false Gospel and your Christ is a pseudo-Christ. I can only plead with you in love: cast away these false revelations and accept the pure teachings of the Bible as God's Word!"

Like that pastor, I too care deeply about "the Bible alone" as our supreme authority. And like him, I worry greatly about wanting to add to the contents of the Scriptures with new "revelations." But for all of that, I don't come to the same harsh depiction of the Mormon Christ as a "pseudo-Christ."

For one thing, in the conversation that we'd been having in this meeting, our Mormon friends didn't say anything about Jesus and his atoning work that contradicted anything in the Bible. Indeed, more often than not, they had actually quoted passages from the New Testament. When they did go beyond biblical appeals to quote from the Book of Mormon, the things they cited said pretty much the same thing that you can find in the Bible.

I've had many hours of discussion of such matters with Mormons, and they've never said in my hearing that their later "revelations" in any way corrected anything in the Bible. Instead, the additional Mormon scriptures are always treated as further elaborations upon — extensions of, supplements to — the contents of the Bible. I may disagree with them on how they understand the relationship of "later" to "earlier"; but in fairness to the Mormons, they don't talk as if the newer revelations somehow supersede the older ones.

Indeed, it has often struck me that their view of their later scriptures is much like my own view of the Calvinist creedal documents that I subscribe to. When I was a member of the Christian Reformed Church, I twice pledged my fidelity to a set of documents that were treated in that denomination as guidelines for understanding the biblical message from the standpoint of Reformed orthodoxy. In doing so, I promised — first when I joined the faculty at Calvin College, and then when I was ordained as an elder in our local congregation — to uphold the truth of, along with the classical Christian creeds, three Reformation-era documents: the Heidelberg Catechism, the Belgic Confession, and the Canons of the Synod of Dort. In subscribing to these documents, I wasn't required to believe that they were "revelations." Rather, I was to treat them as truthful and reliable explanations and clarifications of the teachings of the Bible regarding crucial issues of faith and practice.

I now belong to a mainline Presbyterian denomination in which I hold no "official" office. But I still take those original commitments seriously. I look to those Calvinist documents as my reference point for deciding matters of Reformed orthodoxy. If I come across someone — as I often do — who teaches something that conflicts with the system of thought set forth in those documents, I regard that teaching as less than fully biblical. Does that mean that I treat these documents as on a par with the Bible? Are they further revelations? No, on both counts. But I do see them as containing a reliable *explication of* the biblical message. They have an authority for me that goes beyond the kind of authority that I would attribute to, say, a very fine biblical commentary.

Having said all of that, I must also observe that there are dangers in the view that I've just been setting forth. The difference between standing under the supreme authority of the Bible as God's Word and subscribing to creedal/confessional documents that we take to be reliable "systematizings" of the teachings contained in God's Word isn't always easy to maintain in practice. People who subscribe to extra-biblical creeds and confessions often blur the distinction. And in doing so, we come very close — functionally, if not in theory — to the way Mormons view the relationship between their later scriptures and the Bible.

That's not to say that there's nothing wrong with the way Mormons add to the content of biblical revelation. But to challenge them on this, it's not enough simply to criticize them for treating with great seriousness things that they've added onto the biblical message. We all do that kind of thing. I once had a conversation with a theologian from a "no creed but Christ" church. He explained to me in great detail why his movement opposed creeds. After I had heard him out, I asked him whether anyone could have an official position in his denomination while also insisting that it's a good thing to have a few creeds. He responded with firmness that such a person would not be allowed to hold an office. The explanation he had given me about why creeds were wrong, he said, was the "officially required" teaching of his church. To my ears, that sounded a lot like a creedal requirement!

Catholics and the Development of Dogma

In my arguments with Mormons about the legitimacy of accepting extra-biblical teachings as having the same authority as the contents of the Bible, I'm often reminded of similar discussions that I have with Catholic theologians. For example, Catholicism teaches the doctrine of the immaculate conception of Mary. When I tell my Catholic friends that I can't find that doctrine taught anyplace in the Bible, they agree. It's a later teaching, they argue, but it does have the same kind of "infalli-ble" status as matters that are specifically found in the Bible.

The Catholic understanding of infallible extra-biblical doc-trines, however, differs from the Mormon view in a very signifi-cant way. For Mormonism, the highest office of the church is that of prophet. For Catholicism, the church's highest office is that of teacher — the *magisterium*. This teaching role is exer-cised by thinking carefully about what we've received as revela-tion from God, and drawing out implications.

The extra-biblical teachings of the Catholic Church aren't arrived at by God's directly presenting new revealed truth to the pope. Rather, the pope, normally in concert with other bishops and aided by the theological community, carries forth the task of "the development of dogma." A favorite image em-ployed in this regard is the relationship between seed and flower. The flower doesn't replace or add on to the seed; it is the growing-out of the seed — actualizing that which was there "in" the seed from the beginning. Thus, we can think of the biblical account of the virgin birth of Jesus as the seed, and the doctrine of Mary's immaculate conception as the flower-ing. The church arrives at the latter teaching by reflecting on the former: If Mary was an appropriate instrument that the Holy Spirit used to produce the divine Son, what must Mary have been like? Was she just one more ordinary sinner? Or did God have to prepare her — in the manner, for example, of her own birth — in order to fulfill her assigned role?

I'm explaining the Catholic view, not defending it. I don't endorse the notion of Mary's immaculate conception. But I see the logic of the Catholic argument. And that's the important point — there's a *logic* to it. It's something the Catholic hierar-chy has to substantiate by producing arguments. And if we don't want to endorse the conclusion — the doctrine of the immaculate conception of Mary — then we have to challenge one of the steps along the way, by showing that believing in the virgin birth doesn't compel us to move on from there to the conclusions set forth by the Catholic Church.

All of that is very different from a community that relies on ongoing prophesying. The prophet doesn't link newer teachings to older ones by laying out an argument that establishes continuity. The prophet simply says, "Here is a new word from the Lord."

Organically Continuous with the Bible?

In placing such a strong emphasis on the role of prophets, Mormonism is closer to Pentecostalism than to Catholicism. Pentecostals — along with those in the newer charismatic communities — also often make much of the need for new messages from God. And on occasion these new "revelations" have been viewed as bizarre from the standpoint of historic Christian thought and practice — as when some leader has allegedly been told by God that the world will come to an end on such-and-such a date, or when someone has it on divine authority that a disaster has hit a particular city because of certain sexual sins.

But the mainstream of Pentecostal/charismatic Christianity typically hasn't given credence to such claims. At the very least, new messages from God aren't seen as adding new content to the corpus of biblical truth. Pentecostal prophecies are usually set forth as a restating of biblical teachings for specific contemporary situations, often taking this form: "O my people, says the Lord, do not be discouraged or fearful of what is happening. I am still your God and I will be with you in this time of trouble." Or they may be presented in the form of a specific "word from the Lord" based on prayerful reflection on a specific challenge: "I hear the Lord saying that you should break off this relationship. It is not pleasing to him."

In all of this, the new "revelations" of the Pentecostal/charismatic variety are treated as arising out of biblical revelation. They do not contradict the Bible. And they must in an important sense be "organically" continuous with biblical teachings.

It's precisely at this point that the prophetic office of Mormonism has seemed clearly to diverge from mainstream Christianity in all its forms. An obvious case in point: up until the late 1970s, black men were denied the privileges of priesthood in the LDS. Throughout the civil rights era, the Mormon leadership were constantly challenged to explain their position on this subject, and their constant refrain was that this restriction was a divine mandate and couldn't be changed without a new word from the Lord. That word came in June 1978, when the church's prophet, President Spencer W. Kimball, announced that he had received a revelation that now all worthy males could hold the priesthood.

This raises a key question for Mormonism. On June 1, 1978, it seems that God was continuing his longstanding prohibition regarding black men in the priesthood. Then on the next day, June 2, God was suddenly in favor of blacks in the priesthood. What happened between those two days? Mormon leaders have offered no clear answer to this question. The simple verdict is that on one day God wanted one thing and the next day its opposite.

Now, this is not in itself a strange happening. We all know that changes of practice and doctrinal formulation take place in Christian communities. Catholicism underwent significant changes in this regard as a result of the Second Vatican Council in the early 1960s. And other Christian groups have lifted restrictions on the ordination of women, racial segregation, and so on. But typically these changes come with *rationales* — church leaders sense an obligation to *explain* the shifts. In Mormonism, it seems, no rationale needs to be given. God revealed one thing at a certain point, and then reversed his position without any explanation.

The good news is that this is a matter on which Mormonism seems to be changing. It is not likely that in the future a Mormon prophet will walk into a room to spend time alone with the Lord, and then come out of the room with a new declaration of revelation, without consulting with his counselors in the First Presidency and the Quorum of the Twelve Apostles. The exercise of the office of prophet will happen *communally.* It will emerge out of collective discernment. Discussions about the proposed change will take place — maybe even heated ones — before any proclamation is publicly delivered.

I take that as an important step in the right direction. The prophetic office in Mormonism is taking on more of the character of a teaching office. And the teachings will be arrived at by a communal discussion that takes theological continuity — and especially continuity with the Bible — with utmost seriousness.

To be sure, this is not yet "the Bible alone." But it is at least this: Mormon leadership will add nothing new without being sure that what is accepted as new is continuous with the doctrine of faith, as set forth in Scripture. This, too, means that evangelicals and Mormons have a framework — with at least some shared reference points — for a continuing dialogue about crucial matters of faith.

What about Joseph Smith?

—◦◦◦—

For one of our Mormon-evangelical dialogue sessions, we invited Richard Bushman to talk to us about Joseph Smith. Professor Bushman is a well-known historian of American religion. As a longtime professor of history at Columbia University, he established a reputation as a leading expert on New England Puritanism. He's also a devout Mormon and has written much on the life and thought of Joseph Smith, including his award-winning biography, *Joseph Smith: Rough Stone Rolling*.

In the session we had with him, we asked him to talk to us about Joseph Smith. Most of our dialogue times together are devoted to substantive theological topics, but this time — taking advantage of a noted Joseph Smith scholar — we got into questions about the character of the Mormon founder. At one point, Professor Bushman decided to push back on some of the issues being raised by the evangelicals present. "Is Joseph Smith *possible* for you?" he asked us.

I've thought a lot about that question since. On the face of it, of course, most evangelical Protestants would have an easy time responding to Bushman's challenge. Of course Joseph Smith is possible, they would say; we've seen many like him in the history of religion. All kinds of leaders have emerged who have made wild claims about a special pipeline to God. What else is new? When we come across a person like that, the only question for evangelicals to decide is whether the person is deluded or a charlatan. Or to put it crudely: *a liar or a lunatic?*

Needless to say, Bushman wasn't asking his question in the framework of that kind of simple choice. He was presenting a somewhat different challenge. As a Mormon he was posing a question to longtime critics of the message of Mormonism's prophet: Is *our* Joseph Smith, Bushman was asking — the Joseph Smith who is honored by the Latter-day Saints — is *that* Joseph Smith possible for you? Are you at least open to the *possibility* that God would raise up someone who might occupy a restored prophetic office?

Here, too, of course, many evangelicals would have a ready answer to Bushman's question. And this time the answer would be a straightforward no, he is *not* possible for us. To answer the question in any other way would be for us to concede far more to Mormonism than we're inclined to do. Not only do we deny the truth of Joseph Smith's account of the bringing forth of the Book of Mormon; we also reject those substantive beliefs that have come to be associated with the unique content of Mormon thought: a continuing post-biblical revelation mediated by a living prophet, divine corporeality, eternal progression, and the like — to say nothing of the insistence that much of what we evangelicals hold precious has now been replaced by a "restoration" of a long-lost message.

The Prophet as Possessor of a Creative Imagination?

Our disagreements with Mormons on those matters are serious indeed. It's precisely because I take the disagreements so seriously that I get nervous when some non-Mormon scholars try to find some alternative to the "liar or lunatic" options. Rodney Stark, a sociologist of religion, makes one such attempt. Stark clearly doesn't accept the Mormon perspective on Joseph Smith. At the same time, though, he doesn't want to be forced to choose between what he labels the "psychopathological interpretation," on the one hand, and the insistence, on the other, that Joseph Smith was a "conscious fraud."[1]

So, what would a third way look like? Stark opts for characterizing the Mormon prophet as what he calls a legitimate "revelator." Like many other religious leaders who claim to receive "communications believed to come from a divine being," Stark says, Joseph Smith was possessed of a "creative imagination" that led him to address, with divinely given authority, issues that lie deep in the human experience in a way that speaks to specific historical moments and contexts.[2]

I don't find this line of thought helpful. I agree that religious leaders who manage to attract many followers often utilize a "creative imagination." But when they're imagining that they're receiving messages directly from God, we have to ask whether that "imagination" is serving the cause of truth or falsehood. And if it isn't the truth, then what is motivating them? A sincere but misguided "creative imagina-

1. Rodney Stark, *The Rise of Mormonism,* ed. Reid L. Neilson (New York: Columbia University Press, 2005), 32.
2. Stark, *Rise of Mormonism,* 56.

tion," or imaginings that are consciously designed to deceive others?

When the stakes are as high as they are on matters of dispute between Mormons and traditional Christians, we must be careful to avoid religious relativism. Indeed, simply letting Joseph Smith off the hook by crediting him with a "creative imagination" isn't taking him seriously regarding his own claims about his mission — as well as the claims that many of my Mormon friends make on his behalf. At the core of Mormon teaching is the conviction that Joseph Smith was given something new, directly from the Godhead, a message that trumps all other claims to revealed truth. In the light of what he brought forth, those other systems of religious thought are now to be seen as, if not blatantly false, at least in need of serious correction and revision in the light of the continuing revelations made available to human beings by the reintroduction of living prophets into human affairs.

I see these claims on behalf of Mormonism as at best seriously misleading, much in need of correction and revision in the light of the teachings of the Bible as developed and clarified by historic Christianity. In this sense, then, there's a wide chasm between the evangelical understanding of what we need to know about God's will for humankind and the perspective set forth by Joseph Smith and his followers.

The Mystery of Joseph Smith

Even while I reject the key claims that Joseph Smith made on his own behalf, though, I still struggle to find some way of explaining him — of thinking about Richard Bushman's challenge about the very *possibility* of a Joseph Smith — that gets beyond the simple "liar or lunatic" options. Jan Shipps, a Methodist who has given much scholarly attention to Mormon history, has put it nicely: "the mystery of Mormonism," she says, "cannot be solved until we solve the mystery of Joseph Smith."[3] Like her, I do sense that I'm encountering considerable mystery in my sustained attempts to understand Mormonism in general and Joseph Smith in particular.

I have no delusions about being able to solve the mystery of Joseph Smith here. Indeed, I'm content, in a sense, to live with the mystery. As the Catholic theologian Thomas Weinandy has helpfully commented, theology is best understood as "a mystery discerning enterprise" rather than "a problem solving" one. To solve a problem, he notes, is to make all of our puzzles go away, which is not the kind of resolution that we ought to expect as a matter of course in theological exploration. But we can hope, Weinandy says, to succeed in knowing "more precisely and clearly what the mystery is."[4]

So I won't try to "solve" the mystery of Joseph Smith here. But I do hope that I can say some things that define more clearly the outlines of the mystery. And I want to do that by offering several considerations that can serve to create at least a little bit of space for evangelicals between the "liar or lunatic" options. Such an exercise might allow us to diminish — even if only ever so slightly! — our longstanding unqualified hostility toward Joseph Smith, without in any way sacrificing the strong

3. Jan Shipps, "The Prophet Puzzle," in *The Prophet Puzzle: Interpretive Essays on Joseph Smith,* ed. Bryan Waterman (Salt Lake City: Signature Books, 1999), 43.

4. Thomas G. Weinandy, O.F.M., Cap., *Does God Suffer?* (Notre Dame: University of Notre Dame Press, 2000), 32-34.

theological convictions that have fed that hostility in the past. It may even be that in a modest attempt to clarify the contours of the mystery, we evangelicals may get a clearer grasp of the very real disagreements we have with his perspective on teachings that are so important to our eternal destiny as human beings.

Being Open to God-Given Truths

I've already made it clear that I'm a Calvinist who looks to the Dutch Reformed tradition as a very special guide to theological orthodoxy. I'm especially indebted in this regard to two outstanding theologians in nineteenth-century Holland, Abraham Kuyper and Herman Bavinck. Kuyper did a lot of his theology on the run — he was involved in Dutch politics for over a half-century and served for several years as the Prime Minister of the Netherlands. His colleague, Herman Bavinck, was more the theological scholar, writing hefty volumes on important theological topics.

I had agreed to write a review of one of those Bavinck volumes right around the same time that I was also writing an essay for publication in a volume discussing the life and teachings of Joseph Smith. Since both assignments were due around the same time, I had to engage in a bit of multitasking, switching gears between reading Bavinck for a while and then turning my attention to some aspect of Joseph Smith's career. Going back and forth between Dutch Calvinism and early Mormonism, I had the sense that the two theological worlds had little in common.

But then I came across some comments by Bavinck that struck me as having direct application to my wrestlings with the mystery of Joseph Smith. Writing sometime during the final decades of the nineteenth century, Bavinck was arguing that Calvinists should approach the claims of non-Christian religions with an open mind, referring specifically to Muslim thought:

> In the past the study of religions was pursued exclusively in the interest of dogmatics and apologetics. The founders of [non-Christian] religions, like Mohammed, were simply considered imposters, enemies of God, and accomplices of the devil. But ever since those religions have become more precisely known, this interpretation has proved to be untenable; it clashed both with history and psychology.[5]

While Bavinck apparently knew little or nothing about Mormonism, the relevance of his observations about Mohammed for the case of Joseph Smith seems obvious. Like the Mormon prophet, the founder of Islam also claimed that the contents of his inspired book, the Qur'an, were delivered to him over an extended period of time by an angel, in Mohammed's case Gabriel. And Christianity has a long history of thinkers who responded to Mohammed's claims about his new revelation with arguments designed to show that he was either a liar or a lunatic.

In his comments on the subject, Bavinck refused to carry on in that vein. Indeed, he insisted that it's no longer feasible to dismiss Mohammed simply as one of many "imposters, ene-

5. Herman Bavinck, *Reformed Dogmatics*, vol. 1: *Prolegomena*, trans. John Vriend (Grand Rapids: Baker Academic, 2003), 318.

mies of God, accomplices of the devil" — characterizations
that have also been regularly applied by evangelicals to Joseph
Smith. Instead, Bavinck was encouraging his readers to attend
carefully to the *content* of Mohammed's teachings. And even
more important, he suggested that we can expect to find God-
given truths in those teachings.

Much of the evangelical antipathy toward Joseph Smith has
taken the form of questioning his personal credibility. This
project began in his own day as opponents employed a variety
of strategies to discredit his claims to have received a new revelation. The most careful of these critics have searched diligently for possible sources from which Joseph Smith might
have plagiarized the Book of Mormon. The more strident at-
tacks on his credibility have simply insisted that his message
was inspired by Satan. As an alternative to both of these ap-
proaches, I think the application of Bavinck's suggestion to Joseph Smith makes room for some interesting possibilities.

In order to pursue these possibilities, though, we first have
to pay careful attention to what Bavinck is actually offering us
by way of guidance. For example, when Bavinck observes that
there is "[a]lso among pagans ... a revelation of God," is he telling us that we should expect to find, even in non-Christian
perspectives, straightforward "revealed truths"? It has been
common for proponents of "general revelation" to hold that,
while there are revealed truths that are in some sense "available" to non-Christians, typically the non-Christians — as the
apostle Paul puts it in Romans 1 — "suppress the truth" because of their sinful tendencies. It's one thing, then, to acknowledge the presence of divine revelation "[a]lso among pagans"; it's another thing to see non-Christian thought as
embodying straightforward revealed truths. Nonetheless, rec-

ognition of the positive workings of God beyond the borders of orthodox Christianity should be seen as providing a motivation for careful engagement with other religious perspectives.

Bavinck's observation that Islam has "become more precisely known" is even more poignant now than when he offered it in his nineteenth-century context. For one thing, we've come to understand Islam better as a system of thought. In the early days Islam was seen primarily as a political and military threat — a circumstance wherein it's always tempting to demonize one's enemy. If, however, we're given an opportunity to study and dialogue with the other group's actual teachings in a leisurely manner, we must wrestle with the question of how those teachings have actually inspired deep commitments in the lives of sane people who sincerely accept the teachings.

The shift here is from an agenda shaped by the question "How do we keep them from taking over our world?" to one that emerges when we ask "What is it about their teachings that speaks to what they understand to be their deepest human needs and yearnings?" When we seriously engage the ideas embodied in another religious perspective, participating in give-and-take dialogue with proponents of that perspective, we must also take seriously their own assessment of the founder(s) of their religious community. By carefully examining Islam as a system of thought, for example, we're also forced to consider carefully the way intelligent Muslims view the character of Mohammed. I want to commend the same sort of approach to the present-day assessment of Joseph Smith's teachings.

The Deepest Yearnings of the Human Spirit

I repeat what I said earlier: my own approach to that assessment is to focus on the way in which the religious tradition established by Joseph Smith addresses the deepest yearnings of the human spirit — "the hopes and fears of all the years." This requires, among other things, taking an honest look at the context in which Joseph Smith emerged as a religious leader.

The evangelical historian Nathan Hatch has some helpful observations about this context in his important study of American religious history. Hatch notes that at a time when the young Joseph Smith's family members were experiencing serious illness compounded by financial difficulties, they "looked in vain for solace from the institutional church," which made its presence known in their lives only "in shrill and competing forms."[6] Confronted by "a proliferation of religious options," they underwent — like many of their neighbors — "a crisis of religious authority." In this context, the young Joseph became "convinced that only a new outpouring of divine revelation could pierce the spiritual darkness and confusion that gripped his own soul and that of the modern church."[7]

If we leave aside questions about Joseph Smith's unique character and motivation, the substance of his concern is not an uncommon one. His testimony that the various denominational parties of his day "were equally zealous in endeavoring to establish their own tenets and disprove all others" has a familiar ring, as does his report that "[i]n the midst of this war of

6. Nathan O. Hatch, *The Democratization of American Christianity* (New Haven: Yale University Press, 1989), 113.
7. Hatch, *Democratization*, 114.

words and tumult of opinions, I often said to myself: What is to be done? Who of all these parties are right; or, are they all wrong together? If any one of them be right, which is it, and how shall I know it?"[8] In fact, this kind of puzzlement over how to adjudicate among conflicting theological claims is regularly cited by Protestant converts to Catholicism, in support of their insistence that they have found in the papal authority an anchor for their basic beliefs.[9]

Another historical factor that should be taken into account is the actual manifestation of the Christian tradition against which Joseph Smith was reacting. An important matter in this respect is the doctrine of God that had influenced the spiritual atmosphere of his day.[10] Joseph Smith's Mormonism and Mary Baker Eddy's Christian Science teachings appeared on the scene in the same general period. In their respective metaphysical views — their understandings of the nature of reality — they were exact opposites. Joseph Smith argued that everything is physical, and that even God has a physical body. Mary Baker Eddy, on the other hand, held that everything is spirit, and that the sense that matter is real is a sinful delusion.

Despite their basic differences, though, they shared a common religious motivation. Each of them wanted to bring the

8. Joseph Smith Jr., *History of the Church of Jesus Christ of Latter-day Saints,* ed. B. H. Roberts (Salt Lake City: The Church of Jesus Christ of Latter-day Saints, 1950), 1:9-10.

9. See, for example, the conversion narratives at http://www.chnetwork.org/journals/authority/authority_1.htm.

10. My comments on this subject in the next several paragraphs are a restating of my discussion of this topic in my "Joseph Smith's Theological Challenges: From Revelation and Authority to Metaphysics," in *The Worlds of Joseph Smith: A Bicentennial Conference at the Library of Congress,* ed. John W. Welch (Provo, Utah: Brigham Young University Press, 2006), 218-19.

realm of the divine nearer to the likes of us — to reduce the distance between God and human beings. The founder of Christian Science, for example, would have no difficulty endorsing the Mormon claim that God and human beings are of "the same species," even though she would have a quite different conception of what the "species" consists of metaphysically.

Needless to say, both Joseph Smith and Mrs. Eddy were departing radically from the essential Jewish and Christian teaching that there's a vast metaphysical gap between Creator and creature. But it's one thing to make that point and another for Christians to ask ourselves whether the early-to-mid-nineteenth-century movements that reduced this metaphysical distance can, in any significant way, be seen as a corrective to weaknesses in the sort of Christian theology and practice that were common in their day.

These two "reduce the distance" theologies emerged in an environment shaped significantly by the high Calvinism of New England Puritanism. I think it can be plausibly argued that New England theology, while rightly (from an orthodox Christian perspective) stressing the legitimate *metaphysical* distance between God and his human creatures, nonetheless at the same time fostered an unhealthy *spiritual* distance between the Calvinist deity and his human subjects. Thus it shouldn't surprise us that movements arose to shrink that spiritual distance, even if we must deeply regret that they did so by also shrinking the distance of Being, rather than by drawing on corrective teachings — such as the incarnation and the person of the Holy Spirit — that can be found within orthodox Christian theology. It's not enough for traditional Christians to condemn those movements without also acknowledging the spiritual realities that the dissenting groups were addressing.

Joseph Smith, Cotton Mather, and the "Thin Places"

I want to insert a story here about Cotton Mather, who lived a century or so before Joseph Smith, but who also had an angelic visitation. Mather is a much-respected figure in the evangelical narrative of American religion. Born into a line of Puritan preacher-theologians, he outdid his forebears in the power of his preaching and the brilliance of his theological writings. He's known especially for his condemnations of witchcraft, and if he comes across negatively at all in the minds of evangelical believers it would be because he's viewed as too aggressive in his efforts to uncover any sign of what he took to be Satanic influences in his New England environs.

In this light it's interesting to note that in the early autumn of 1693, Mather, a thirty-year-old still struggling to understand God's calling in his life, had an encounter with the supernatural that, he testified, had a profound impact on his spiritual development. Mather was fascinated with biblical reports of angelic interventions in human affairs, and he devoted much attention, in the form of intense spiritual struggle, to the possibility of a continuing connection of human beings with divine messengers. Then one day, in the privacy of his bedroom, he experienced what he came to describe as a "strange and memorable thing":

> After outpourings of prayer, with the utmost fervor and fasting, there appeared an Angel, whose face shone like the noonday sun. He was completely beardless, but in other respects human, his head encircled by a splendid tiara. On his shoulders were wings; his garments were white and shining; his robe reached to his ankles; and

about his loins was a belt not unlike the girdles of the peoples of the East.[11]

Mather didn't record the details of the message that the angel delivered to him, but he did testify that the angel prophesied that he, Cotton Mather, would accomplish great things, and that his intellectual influence would reach to the European continent.[12]

Kenneth Silverman, who provides this account in his biography of Cotton Mather, observes that "[a]s a Puritan . . . Cotton Mather was born into a society that daily felt the nearness of the invisible world and wove magical and supernatural notions into the very texture of his thinking, beginning in childhood."[13] In offering this observation about the mood of the time, Silverman is giving a sympathetic portrayal of Mather's account of the angelic visitation without thereby endorsing that account as literally true. Mather lived in a time when the expectation of such experiences was not uncommon. In reporting such an encounter in his own life, he need not be seen as either a deliberate deceiver or a deluded fool. There's too much in the rest of the story of Mather's spiritual pilgrimage simply to force him into one of the two "liar or lunatic" categories. We can continue to puzzle over what "really" happened that led him to insist on the truth of his story about the angel's visit, while continuing to appreciate — and even benefit from — his overall contribution.

11. Mather didn't record this in his diary, but in a separate document, and he described the visitation in Latin. The translation here is by Kenneth Silverman, *The Life and Times of Cotton Mather* (New York: Harper and Row, 1984), 127-28.

12. Silverman, *Cotton Mather*, 128.

13. Silverman, *Cotton Mather*, 129.

Silverman's observation about the spiritual influences that shaped Cotton Mather can be extended to Joseph Smith in at least this regard: in the Mormon founder's environment, too, the expectation of supernatural visitations was not uncommon. Indeed, the worlds of Joseph Smith and Cotton Mather weren't far removed from each other temporally and geographically.

Commentators on Celtic spirituality often refer to the phenomenon of "thin places," usually linked particularly to Ireland. These are spaces or regions where, as one writer puts it, "the veil between this world and the next is so sheer that it is easy to step through."[14] To be sure, the way in which Joseph Smith made use of his testimony to the stepping-through of the veil is very different from the use to which Cotton Mather put his visitation — Mather certainly saw nothing in his encounter with the angel that undercut the sole authority of the Bible. Nonetheless, perhaps something of the evangelical hostility toward Joseph Smith could be diminished, at least to some small degree, by reflecting in more general terms on what it might mean for persons to live in the "thin places," in times and places where the veil between worlds is taken to be a fact of life.

The Danger of Stark Alternatives

I said early on that I wouldn't solve the mystery of Joseph Smith but that I hoped at least to offer some probings that might allow evangelicals to discern the mystery more clearly.

14. C. Wayne Hilliker, "Seeing God as God Is," *The Chalmers Pulpit*, http://www.chalmersunitedchurch.com/sermons/oct17s99.htm.

The considerations I've set out briefly here may help some in that effort. They may allow us to make a little space for Joseph Smith between the "liar or lunatic" poles. But the moves I've been proposing will have little real effect apart from a disposition on the part of evangelicals to *look* for that kind of space.

The problem is that some evangelicals have a tendency — especially when we're asked to assess the differences between different worldviews — to see things in terms of stark alternatives. A perspective on life is either righteous or unrighteous. Every moral option is either right or wrong. You're either on God's side or Satan's. And a person like Joseph Smith is either a true prophet of God or a deceiver — with the only point worth debating being whether he was a liar or a lunatic.

The tendency to reduce the situation to simple alternatives in the case of Joseph Smith is reinforced by a legitimate antipathy toward the Mormon teaching that humans and the members of the Godhead belong to the same order of being. As I mentioned earlier, this claim flies in the face of the traditional understanding of biblical teaching, that God is God and we are not, and that any effort to close the metaphysical gap runs the clear risk of espousing idolatry.

Idolatry is indeed a very bad thing, and it's a good thing to take a strong stand against it. But I repeat here G. K. Chesterton's wise counsel: setting up false gods is a terrible thing, but wrongly to demonize a person who is not a demon is also bad, and evangelicals have to be careful not to sin against Joseph Smith and his followers by setting up false devils.

A Shared Humanity

Evangelicals have often thought of their approach to Mormonism as a form of spiritual warfare. Insofar as this combat imagery creates an atmosphere wherein those evangelicals who want to engage in genuine dialogue with Mormons are seen as traitors to the cause, the use of such imagery is regrettable. But since the encounter between Mormonism and evangelical Christianity is indeed one between conflicting systems of thought, something like the "just war" recommendations that I cited earlier from John Calvin can be given helpful application here. It would be a healthy spiritual exercise for evangelicals to examine our own motives in the ways we've portrayed Joseph Smith, making sure we haven't been "carried away with headlong anger" or "seized with hatred." And Calvin's recommendation about having "pity on the common nature" we share with our opponents — as applied to dealing with serious religious differences — can be seen as a plea for empathy toward those with whom we disagree. We must never lose sight of the basic features of human nature that we share, even with our worst enemies.

Indeed, it's this factor of a shared human bonding that motivates me to wrestle seriously with the ideas set forth in Joseph Smith's perspective on religious matters, even though I continue to reject his claims to have received a new revelation from the heavens. In my conversations with Mormon friends, particularly those who have studied carefully Joseph Smith's life and teachings, I've been impressed by two things, one that gives me discomfort and another that gives me comfort. The discomfort is to be expected, given our basic disagreements: they see Joseph Smith as a prophet and a restorer and I do not. But the factor that brings me comfort caught me up short when I first encountered it, although I've now come to expect it. It's the candor with which my Mormon friends empathetically treat Joseph Smith as a very human person — "warts and all," as one of them once put it. They treat him with the kind of affection and respect that also has room for acknowledging flaws, and even serious mistakes in behavior and teaching.

It's precisely this willingness on their part to engage in a nuanced discussion of Joseph Smith's worldview that inspires me to continue in the conversation. Like me, they see the question about how a human being can be reconciled with the Eternal as the most important issue anyone can face. The fact is that Joseph Smith articulated a perspective on this topic that has captured the imaginations of millions of people who have become his followers. However we might assess the question of the "possibility" of a Joseph Smith, then, there's no doubt in my mind that the ideas he set forth can serve as an important springboard for ongoing conversation about matters that go deep into the secret places of our shared humanity.

Cutting Some Slack

—⟨⟩⟨⟩⟨⟩—

Not too long after our Mormon-evangelical dialogues began, I invited my co-director of the conversations, BYU professor Robert Millet, to speak to the Board of Trustees at Fuller Theological Seminary. I had kept the trustees — the group to whom I'm directly accountable as Fuller's president — aware of what we had initiated in this new venture, and I wanted them to hear firsthand from an important Mormon leader about his perspective on the project. None of the Fuller trustees had raised any serious objections to what we were doing. But they were understandably curious, and maybe even a little nervous about something that could easily become controversial in our broader evangelical constituency.

Bob was his usual winsome self, and the trustees came away from that encounter fully supportive of the dialogues. One thing he said that evening was especially compelling. He said he was thankful that Fuller was willing to take the risks in co-sponsoring these conversations with Mormon scholars. "We need a safe place to talk honestly with each other," he said.

"We Mormons have basically been out of touch with any kind of serious conversations with representatives of historic Christianity for a century-and-a-half. We don't always know whether we're actually using the right theological terminology in trying to clarify our teachings. So my plea is simple: Cut us a little slack!"

I keep wanting to repeat Bob Millet's plea to evangelicals who are quick to question the whole enterprise of dialogue with Mormons. Some send me angry emails and snail mail letters. "How can you take these Mormons seriously, and even *hint* that some of them might be genuine Christians? Don't you know what they believe? God has a body. Jesus and Satan are brothers. Mormons are on their way to becoming gods." And so on. Then some people give me reading assignments. If only I would read what Walter Martin taught about Mormonism, or would digest what Ed Decker and Dave Hunt wrote about "the God-makers," or would take seriously what this or that ex-Mormon has reported about what Mormonism is like "on the inside."

After writing the previous paragraph, I stopped to check my email. The newest message on my screen was from "Don," who was upset with me about something I had written about our Mormon-evangelical dialogues. It was as if Don had decided to offer an illustration of the phenomenon I was writing about at that very moment:

Mr. Mouw:

I was a member of the mormon church and now an evangelical christian. Frankly, you are mistaken . . . dangerously mistaken in my view. Mormonism is a cult. How do I know? I lived it for many years. What mormons like the deceitful Bob Millett will tell you in public and what mormons talk about in private are two very different things. You are being beguiled by a church that is expert in pulling the wool over people's eyes.

What can I say to people like Don? Probably nothing that will convince them. But neither am I prepared to heed their warnings. When it comes to how best to understand Mormon teachings, I'm certainly open to correction. But do I honestly think I've been systematically duped by the Mormon friends with whom I've been in sustained contact over a decade or so?

I have a difficult time even entertaining that thought, and for a very good reason. For a number of years now, I've not only paid close attention to what Mormons say to me and my fellow evangelicals in lengthy discussions, but also paid close attention to what they say to each other. I've witnessed many occasions where my Mormon friends argue with each other, rather passionately at times, about important points of doctrine. Nothing in those exchanges even remotely resembles a "rehearsed" performance designed to deceive evangelicals.

A more significant case in point: Elder Jeffrey Holland, one of the LDS General Authorities, not only has talked privately with some of us about the ways in which LDS leaders are placing a much stronger emphasis these days on the "finished work" of the atoning sacrifice of Jesus Christ on the Cross of Calvary, as well as the need for fallen sinners to rely completely on the grace of God for salvation; he and his colleagues have also publicly preached that kind of message in unambiguous terms to tens of thousands of Mormons in their addresses in recent years at the annual General Conferences. The evidence is available to anyone who has access to YouTube![1]

False Choices

A friend told me about a time when, back in the 1960s, he was asked, as a recent college graduate bound for seminary studies, to address his home congregation — an all-white congregation in the Midwest — about his hopes for studying for the ministry. One thing he mentioned to the congregation was his desire to be more effective as a Christian in working for racial reconciliation, specifically between whites and blacks.

An older member of the congregation was very upset with him for bringing up the issue of race. "You don't really know what these colored people are like," the man told him. "I hope seminary will cure you of these liberal ideas!"

Three years later that same congregation invited my friend to preach. In his sermon he shared with the congregation some positive experiences about racial reconciliation that he'd had during an extensive student internship that he'd recently served at an all-black inner-city church. Afterward, the same church member was once again critical of what he said about race relations, but this time his complaint was different: "You're just saying all these nice things about the colored people because you've spent so much time with them. You aren't capable of being objective!"

My friend found this very frustrating. It's one of those "you can't win" situations. Either your views about a group are

1. A fine example is at http://www.youtube.com/watch?v=yr6Un5XpFZU.

judged to be based on *inadequate* experience with the group, or you're seen as having *too much* experience. You're either ignorant or duped.

I've felt that same kind of frustration recently with regard to my relation to the LDS. Some critics insist that I simply don't understand Mormonism. Others see the long-term dialogue itself as the real problem. You know them too well, these people tell me. Having spent all those hours with Mormon scholars and church leaders has dulled your ability to see things clearly. They've duped you. Now you're one of their apologists. One blogger put it this way: Mouw has spent so much time with the Mormons, he said, that "he has finally gone native!"

"You don't really know them" and "You know them too well" are false choices. The alternative in any relationship with people with whom we disagree about serious issues is to listen carefully and patiently, asking questions, discerning patterns of thought. The goal of all this is not simply to understand — although that's a worthy goal. It's to earn the trust that allows genuine dialogue about our deepest convictions. For me and my house that means hoping for the opportunity to talk about the Savior.

Hopeful Signs for Dialogue

Spencer Fluhman is a young Mormon scholar who recently earned his Ph.D. and is now a history professor at Brigham Young University. A participant in our Mormon-evangelical dialogue, Spencer converses easily with evangelicals, showing a willingness to entertain new — and old! — questions in a self-critical spirit. There's no question about his fidelity to his Mormon faith, but he also clearly wants to link his Mormon convictions to what he sees as the deep concern in the Christian tradition to acknowledge the supremacy of Jesus Christ as Lord and Savior.

I know that what I've just written about him won't sit well with many of my fellow evangelicals. "Your friend," they'll say, "can't have it both ways. It's either his Mormon convictions or the true Christ. He must choose!"

That's not my assessment. I see Spencer as one of the many hopeful signs within Mormonism. Given his historical instincts, in fact, he can often be found defending what I regard as Mormonism's less orthodox elements in our meetings. But he wants to keep talking about these things, and so do I.

In a recent volume of essays about Joseph Smith's career, published by BYU's Religious Study Center, Spencer contributed a lengthy scholarly essay on the developing ideas about "church government" from the LDS's early days to the present. He treats many issues that make people like me nervous about Mormon belief and practice: Joseph Smith's various visions, Mormon priesthood, the office of prophet, baptismal regeneration, temple ordinances, and so on.

All of this he treats with an obvious love of his tradition. As he draws to a close, though, he quotes something from Joseph Smith that I've often cited in discussions with Mormons — a line that I wish they'd expound upon more diligently. Here's the line: "And we know that justification through the grace of our Lord and Savior Jesus Christ is just and true" (Doctrines and Covenants, 20:29-30).

John Calvin and Martin Luther, Spencer observes, would have been pleased to hear that from the lips of the Mormon prophet. And Spencer fully endorses that expression. Even when defending the Mormon emphasis on priesthood and the ordinances, he cautions against viewing either apart from Christ's redemptive power. "In my mind," he remarks, "participation in the ordinances of the Church does not *earn* salvation for the Saints. . . . No decision, no earthly work, no human striving could possibly *merit*" what we receive from Christ's atoning work. And then this:

> Does any Latter-day Saint think that the accumulated righteousness of a lifetime could deserve *that?* Theologically speaking, it just does not add up. No, Latter-day Saints stand with the rest of Christendom, "all amazed . . . [and] confused at the grace he so fully proffers" us. . . . His [Jesus'] unmatched gifts are just that: gifts. And no one earns gifts.[2]

I read this shortly before a theological conference at which some Protestant theologians were discussing issues of salvation. One of them explicitly denied the very point that Spencer was making in the comments I just quoted. This liberal theologian wanted nothing to do with a salvation that was made possible only by the free grace that sent the Savior to shed his blood at Calvary. That denial made me eager to get back to my dialogues with my Mormon friends!

---

2. J. Spencer Fluhman, "Authority, Power, and the 'Government of the Church of Christ,'" in *Joseph Smith: The Prophet and Seer,* ed. Richard Neitzel Holzapfel and Kent P. Jackson (Provo, Utah: Religious Studies Center, Brigham Young University, 2010), 225-26.

Knowing Lincoln, Knowing Jesus

—◦◦◦—

I think often about an illustration I heard many times in my childhood from preachers, especially those who functioned as traveling evangelists. I heard the illustration so often that I've wondered whether there's some book of sermon illustrations somewhere to which it could be traced. The three key characters in the story were always the same: Abraham Lincoln, a present-day scholar who has studied Lincoln's presidency, and a little girl who lived next door to Mr. Lincoln.

The story began with the present-day scholar. He has studied all that is available to know about the facts of Lincoln's presidency, the preacher would report. The details of the Lincoln-Douglas debates, different stages of Lincoln's thinking about slavery, the daily events of the Civil War, arguments Lincoln had with his advisors — this scholar had researched it all. But, of course, as a present-day professor he had never met Lincoln personally.

The little girl, on the other hand, knew nothing about Lincoln's official role. She didn't even realize that he was such an important person. But every day, when Lincoln would leave his home to go off to his important duties, he would see the little girl playing in front of her home and would go over to wish her a good day. He would sometimes stop to talk to her. Often he would sing a song with her. And he would give her a brief hug. The little girl didn't know the facts about Lincoln — but she knew his warm embrace.

The preacher would then ask us in the congregation: Who knew Lincoln better? The scholar who had all of the facts right but had never met Lincoln personally? Or the little girl who couldn't say much about the facts of Lincoln's leadership, but nonetheless knew his loving embrace?

It was always clear to me that the preacher expected us to decide for the little girl. And the application to what it means to have a relationship with Jesus was also very clear. We could be good church people, able to say all of the right things doctrinally. But unless we knew the Savior's warm embrace, none of the other things really counted on the question of our eternal destiny.

I still accept the point of that illustration. To be sure, I would insist on nuancing it a little differently, as an evangelical who wants to be sure that the overall case gets put accurately. The scholar who knew all of the facts about Lincoln did possess an important kind of knowledge. And one could hope that the little girl, when she grew older, would want to enrich her experiential awareness of Lincoln with some grasp of the nature of his public leadership.

But the basic point still stands. And it fits the pattern of my own life. My earliest awareness of Jesus was that he loves me — "for the Bible tells me so." That love — the Savior's warm embrace — has stayed with me over the years, even as I've worked at studying "all the facts about him." Indeed, that early experience of the love of Jesus has been undergirded and sustained through difficult times by attempts at careful thinking about who Jesus is and how he exercises his authority as Savior and Lord.

There have been times along the way in my adult life when I've changed my views about this or that aspect of the nature and person of Jesus Christ. Sometimes I've looked back at my previous ideas and realized I was moving in dangerous directions theologically. But through all of that, the presence of Jesus in my life has stayed pretty much the same. I've always experienced him as a loving Savior who offers me his warm embrace.

The basic point of the sermon illustration of my childhood, then, still holds for me. A person can fall far short of a robust theological orthodoxy and still be in a genuine relationship with Jesus. It's not that doctrine — careful theological formulation — is unimportant. We have to work hard at that, if we want to have our relationship with the Lord solidly grounded in the truth. I have to remind myself of that in my own life constantly. And I also like engaging in that important theological work with my Mormon friends.